FURNITURE FUNDAMENTALS
Chairs & Benches

POPULAR WOODWORKING BOOKS

CINCINNATI, OHIO

popularwoodworking.com

Contents

Greene & Greene Garden Bench

BY JIM STUARD

This understated garden bench is like no other we've seen. The fluid lines of the top and sides are inspired by the architectural work of the Greene brothers, who built houses and furniture around the turn of the century that are fast becoming national treasures. Yet this bench is surprisingly simple to build and will quickly catch the eye of everyone who visits your garden or solarium.

We used genuine mahogany for the bench, though you could easily substitute oak, teak or any other wood suitable for outdoors. (If you plan to use teak, be prepared to open that checkbook wide.) We bought our lumber already planed and surfaced. Purchasing rough stock would knock 30 percent to 40 percent off the price.

Start by laying out your crosscuts on the lumber. Because there are a lot of pieces to this bench, I marked each piece with a letter. Crosscut the lumber to rough length on a radial arm saw.

Take the wood to your jointer and edge joint one edge of each piece. This will give you a square, straight edge for ripping. Rip out the pieces at your table saw and then crosscut to the finished lengths in the Schedule of Materials.

Build the Back
Attaching the slats to the top cap and the bottom back rail requires a little math to get evenly spaced slats. You have 14 narrow slats that are $1^1/2$" wide, and three wider slats that are $2^1/2$" wide. The bottom back rail is 48" long. So subtract 21" from that 48" length to account for the small slats, and then subtract $7^1/2$" to account for the wide slats. This should leave you with $19^1/2$" for the spacing. Then divide this number by 16, which is the number of openings between the slats. This leaves $1^7/32$" between each slat.

Next, you need to lay out the slat locations on the top cap and bottom back rail. Here's how: Start at one end of the back rail and measure in $2^1/2$" in from the end for the wider slats. Then measure out $1^7/32$" of space, then $1^1/2$" for the slat, then $1^7/32$" and so on until you've laid out seven narrow slats. Then start from the other side of the rail and lay out those seven narrow slats. The wider center slat is centered in what's left. The wider slats

Using a rule with at least $^1/32$" increments, lay out the locations for the dowel and biscuit cuts. Then, using a self-centering doweling jig, drill the $^1/4$" dowel holes in the slats (two per slat end). Make sure the holes are just a shade deeper than the dowels you plan to use. This gives room for your glue to move.

will be attached with biscuits; the narrow slats with dowels. To find the dowel centers on the back rail, measure in $^1/4$" from the marks you made for the ends of each narrow slat. Drill the holes for the dowels on the bottom back rail as shown in the photo. Then lay out the holes on the top cap, keeping in mind it is 1" longer than the bottom back rail.

Cloud Lifts
Cut the cloud lift pattern on the top cap using the pattern in the diagram and

a band saw. (Cloud lifts are soft, stair-stepped details.) Then cut the reverse cloud lift pattern on the apron that attaches to the front of the seat, as shown in the photo.

Straighten the Pattern
After you rough-cut the cloud lift shape on the band saw, straighten up the cuts on the table saw. When you're cleaning up the reverse cloud lift pattern, you need to be careful because you're going to have to raise and lower the table saw blade to

Who Were the Greenes?
Charles Sumner Greene (1869–1957) and Henry Mather Greene (1870–1954) designed some of the most sought-after houses and custom furniture in the Pasadena, California, area. The brothers were born in Brighton, Ohio, and studied woodworking, metalworking and toolmaking at Washington University in St. Louis. After studying architecture at the Massachusetts Institute of Technology and a short stint as apprentices to other architects, Charles and Henry moved to Pasadena and set up their own architectural firm. On their trip West, the two stopped at the Columbian Exposition in Chicago and saw Japanese architecture for the first time, which greatly influenced both brothers.

Unlike many of their Arts & Crafts contemporaries, the Greene brothers' furniture and interiors were designed using teak and mahogany instead of quartersawn white oak. Their work also has a decidedly Japanese flavor not found in the works of Gustav Stickley and the Roycrofters.

The Greene brothers' most famous design is the Gamble House in Pasadena. Commissioned in 1908 by David Berry Gamble (of Procter & Gamble fame), the house was once in danger of being sold to a family that planned to paint the stunning mahogany and teak interiors white. The house is now operated as a museum.

get into the middle of the pattern. To finish the cloud lift pattern, use a $1/4$" round-over bit to cut a profile on the edges.

Assemble the Back

Now you have to do a little sanding. Using #120-grit sandpaper and a random orbital sander, sand the flat surfaces and break the edges of the back's slats. This will, in the end, give the piece a more finished look. It also has a practical purpose. If your bench is going to sit outside, the first spring shower or two will raise the grain of the wood. Squared edges will likely splinter, making your bench a potentially painful place to sit.

Attach the wider slats with biscuits; the narrower ones with dowels. Make your cuts for the biscuits on the wider slats and the back rails. After dry assembling the back, start with the bottom rail. Paint your dowels with waterproof glue and insert them into the back rail. Then paint the other dowels' ends with glue and put a little glue on the end of the slat. Attach the slats. Then glue the dowels into the top back rail. Paint them with glue, put a little glue on the top end of each slat and attach the top rail. Clamp and let dry.

Cut Out the Square Patterns

The four-square pattern that goes on the back is repeated on the center stiles on the end. Mark the locations of the cutouts according to the diagram and lay out the location of the four squares.

First lay out the cloud lifts with a compass. Use a 1" Forstner bit to cut the inside radius on the top, apron and armrests (use a $1/2$" bit for the cloud lifts on the end pieces).

Drill holes to make the pattern using a $1/2$" Forstner bit. Clean up the holes with a jigsaw and a chisel.

Build the Ends

Begin building the ends by cutting the cloud lift and reverse cloud lift patterns on the top, bottom and middle rails with a band saw. Use the $1/4$" roundover bit on all the edges except those on the inside of the sides; these will be radiused after assembly.

Next make the cuts for your biscuits. These will attach the center stiles to the rails, and attach the rails to the legs. Make sure the rails and the legs are flush

After you rough out the cloud lifts on a band saw, use a table saw to rip to the bottom of the inside radius cut on the drill press. (On the reverse cloud lifts for the apron, you need to set the ripping width with the table saw blade lowered below the table. With the saw running, hold the work firmly in place, making sure your hand is clear of the point where the blade will exit the piece. Then slowly raise the blade to make the interior cuts.) Then use your band saw to remove the waste on the outside radii. Clean up the cuts on a spindle sander.

Greene & Greene Garden Bench

LET.	NO.	ITEM	DIMENSIONS (INCHES)			MATERIAL
			T	W	L	
A	3	Seat braces	$3/4$	3	$17^5/8$	Mahogany
B	8	Seat slats	$3/4$	2	48	Mahogany
C	1	Angled slat for seat	$3/4$	$1^3/4$	48	Mahogany
D	1	Seat front apron	$3/4$	5	48	Mahogany
E	4	Legs	$1^3/8$	3	$24^5/8$	Mahogany
F	4	Upper & lower side rails	$3/4$	3	$15^3/4$	Mahogany
G	2	Middle side rails	$3/4$	4	$15^3/4$	Mahogany
H	4	Center side stiles	$3/4$	2	$5^5/8$	Mahogany
I	2	Armrests	$3/4$	3	23	Mahogany
J	1	Top cap	$1^1/4$	5	49	Mahogany
K	2	Back bottom rail	$3/4$	4	48	Mahogany
L	3	Wide back slats	$3/4$	$2^1/2$	15	Mahogany
M	14	Narrow back slats	$3/4$	$1^1/2$	15	Mahogany
N	1	Seat back rail	$3/4$	$2^3/8$	48	Mahogany

on the inside edge where they will attach to the seat. Use waterproof glue with the biscuits; clamp and set aside to dry.

Rout the Edges

When dry, use your router to radius the edges of the ends. Then cut out the armrests to the pattern shown in the diagram. Attach them to the end assemblies with screws, leaving an $1/8$" overhang on the inside edge and notch the arm to the back.

Seat Assembly

The first thing to do here is to cut out the three seat braces that support the seat's slats. Cutting the braces is a little tricky because there are several angles at work here. Once you've got the seat braces cut, make the seat's back rail. This piece runs along the entire back of the bench and is the place where the bench's back and the seat are joined.

To make the back tip at a comfortable angle, cut a bevel on both edges of this piece. Set the angle of your table saw's blade to 7°. Run one edge through. Then flip the piece over lengthwise and run the other edge through, creating a parallel cut to the first one.

While you're at the table saw, set the blade's angle to 10°. Take the $1^1/2$" wide seat slat and run one edge through the saw to create a bevel. Then flip the piece onto its other face and run the other edge through. The result is one face that is narrower than the other. This seat slat goes on the highest part of the seat, and the bevel will make the seat more comfortable.

Then, using screws and waterproof glue, attach the three seat braces to the seat's back rail. Then take one of the 2" slats for the seat and attach it to the front of the three seat braces with screws and waterproof glue. Screw and glue the rest

DETAILS OF CLOUD LIFT RADII

DETAIL A

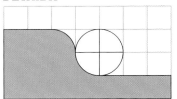

DETAIL B

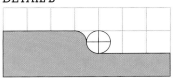

Each square = $1/2$"

Enlarge 200%

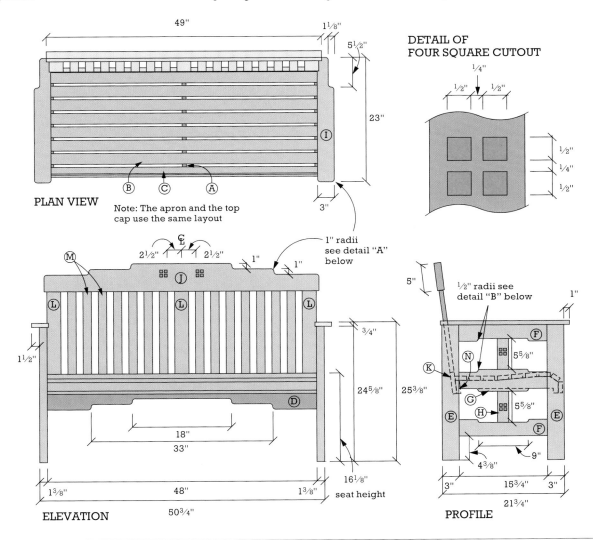

PLAN VIEW

Note: The apron and the top cap use the same layout

DETAIL OF
FOUR SQUARE CUTOUT

ELEVATION

PROFILE

of the slats as shown in the photo, making sure to attach the beveled 1½" slat to the highest point of the seat.

Notch the Apron

When I designed the front apron, I intended it to be merely decorative. However, after some experimentation, I decided it could help hold up the seat. To attach it to the seat, cut three ¾" × 2" notches into the front rail and screw the front rail into the seat behind the front rail. Use a sharp chisel to cut a screw pocket on the back face of the apron near each end. This is where you will attach the apron to the legs.

Assembly

Screw the back bottom rail to the seat's back rail with eight screws. Place one of the bench's end assemblies flat on the floor. Using a square, measure where the seat brace attaches to the seat's side rail and mark a line. Then mark three biscuit cuts that will attach the back leg to the end of the back. Mark both sides of the back on the leg.

Attach the Ends

Attach the seat assembly to the back leg with biscuits. Then, from the inside of the bench, screw the seat brace to the seat's side rail using 1¼" screws. Be careful not to countersink too much, or the screw will go through both thicknesses of wood.

Then screw the apron to the leg in the screw pocket you cut earlier using a 1⅝" galvanized screw. Repeat this procedure for the other side assembly. You can finish this bench with varnish or an outdoor-safe polyurethane. I chose to leave the wood bare so it will slowly turn a silvery gray.

This bench looks great in the garden or solarium and will last for years outdoors, but some of you might opt to keep yours in the front hall or near the back door.

Dry-assemble the back to make sure everything lines up and that the back can be made square. Then, using clamping cauls, assemble the back with a waterproof glue (we used polyurethane glue). Check for square by measuring across the corners. The measurements should be identical. Then adjust the clamps accordingly.

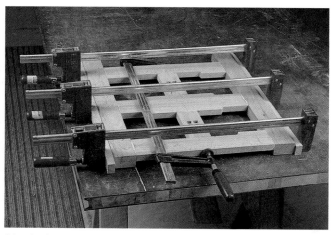

After laying out the ends and cutting the cloud lifts on these parts, mark the pieces for the biscuit jointer cuts. Assemble the stiles and the rails first. With this assembly clamped loosely, clamp the legs on and allow to dry (urethane glue takes about four hours to dry and has a foamy squeeze-out).

After the ends are dry, use a ½" roundover bit to radius all of the edges – except the top where the armrest will be attached. Using a four-in-hand rasp and starting at a 45° angle to the corner, gently file out a mitered corner. Remove burn marks from the corners with the rasp and finish the corners with sandpaper.

After the slats are screwed in, flip the seat over and lay the front apron against the front slat. Mark the locations of the seat braces onto the apron. Using a backsaw and chisel, cut 2" × 3/4" notches into the apron. Attach the apron to the back of the front slat with screws and glue. You also need to cut a 7/8" × 16" cutaway into the ends of the seat braces. This starts at the back of the seat brace and keeps the seat brace from peeking below the cloud lift on the ends.

The diagram in the plans shows the shape of the three seat braces. Attach the tapered seat slat to the front angle on the seat brace. Then, using galvanized screws, attach the remaining seat slats, leaving about 7/16" between each slat.

Clamp a straight piece of wood to the front line on the leg. Then using a biscuit jointer with the fence removed, make your biscuit cuts.

Clamp the seat assembly to the back, making sure the back is flush to the bottom of the seat. Screw the two together with 1 1/4" galvanized screws and glue. Then, on the inside of the ends, lay out the location of the seat braces. The seat brace starts 13" up from the bottom of the leg to the inside of the cutaway explained in the top right photo on the page.

Greene & Greene Hall Bench

BY JIM STUARD

This will upset some of the purists out there, but I think that some of the best designs in the Arts & Crafts style came from the fringes of the movement. Instead of Gustav Stickley's massive and square forms, I prefer art nouveau-influenced furniture from Scotsman Charles Rennie Mackintosh. And instead of the squarish Lifetime furniture, I've always liked the Asian influence in the furniture and architecture of Charles and Henry Greene.

This bench from the brothers Greene was designed and built in 1907 for the Robert R. Blacker house in Pasadena, California. The story behind this house is a sad one. As the furniture designed for the house went out of style, most of it was sold at a yard sale in 1947. Then, in 1985, the house was purchased and within three days was stripped of most of its lighting fixtures, stained glass windows and door transoms. These were sold piecemeal to collectors all over the world, quickly recouping the $1 million price of the house. Though new owners have taken possession of the house and a strong effort is being made to reclaim the original pieces, many can only be seen in photos, or as reproductions.

This bench is as faithful to the original as I could manage, including the reed-like design of the back slats that lend a lightness not often seen in the Arts & Crafts style. The construction is a blend of modern and traditional. And while the original was made of teak, I chose cherry.

The Case of the Chair

Because this project is a mix of case construction and chair building, you'll use techniques from both disciplines. Begin construction by cutting the parts according to the cutting list. The most difficult step is getting the joint between the back legs and top rail right. It's a specialized coped-miter that requires patience.

The front legs can be cut from 8/4 material, while the back legs are cut from a laminated blank glued up using scarf joints (see the diagrams for details). I used three pieces of 8/4 cherry for each back leg, with the back section cut from the longest piece to avoid showing a visible seam. Start shaping the legs by cutting the profile first. Cut the top radius on the back

leg after the back is assembled. Next cut the outside radius of each back leg on the elevation face. Before cutting the curve on the inside edge, lay out and cut the coped miter for the top rail according to the diagram. The straight inside edge gives a better reference for laying out the coped miter. Then rout a $\frac{1}{4}$" radius on the visible corners of all the legs. Now cut out the arms on the band saw.

To form the storage area, the box ends need a 6° bevel on the front and back edges, and a $\frac{1}{4}$" × $\frac{1}{4}$" groove for the bottom that's cut $\frac{1}{2}$" up from the lower inside edge. The same groove is necessary on the front and back box pieces.

After making these cuts, mark and cut biscuit slots to attach the front and back legs to the box ends. Make the slots to hold the end panels recessed $\frac{1}{2}$" in from the outside of each leg.

The next step is to cut a $\frac{1}{4}$" × $\frac{3}{4}$" tenon on the top end of the boards from which the back slats will be cut. On the bottom end of the boards, cut a 7° bevel to allow the slats to lean to the back, so the long part of the bevel should face forward. Next, cut out the slat shapes on a band saw and use a scroll saw for the centers of the two spade-shaped slats. Then clean up the rough edges with a spokeshave.

The templates for the slats are provided on the scaled-down grids. After enlarging them, lay out the templates on your wood, cut the tenons on the ends of the boards and band saw the slats to shape.

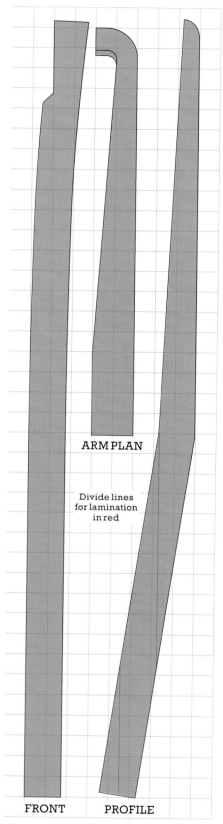

ARM PLAN

Divide lines
for lamination
in red

FRONT   PROFILE

**FRONT/PROFILE OF BACK LEG
AND ARM PLAN**
Each square = 1"

While the slats can be sanded smooth, I find that a spokeshave helps remove irregularities left by the band saw. It also gives the piece a hand-worked appearance.

Notching the back leg to fit the back rail is a little tricky, so take the time to do it right. This joint is one of the most noticed features of the piece.

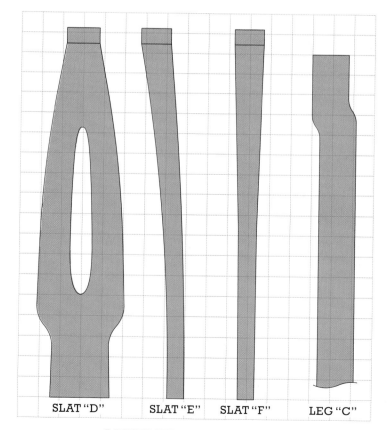

SLAT "D"   SLAT "E"   SLAT "F"   LEG "C"

BACK SLATS AND LEG PROFILE
Each square = 1"

I made a simple mortising jig to help with the bread-boards. Once the three-piece jig is done, a plunge router makes simple work of the mortises.

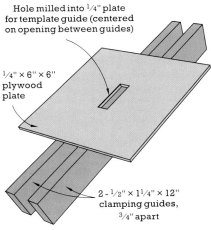

Hole milled into ¼" plate for template guide (centered on opening between guides)

¼" × 6" × 6" plywood plate

2 - ½" × 1¼" × 12" clamping guides, ¾" apart

MORTISING JIG

Making Ends Meet

You're now ready to dry-assemble the bench frame. Use biscuits again to attach the box front and box back between the legs. Make sure the angles are correct and the bottom fits. Then cut the top rail to length and clip the corners at a 45° angle to fit between the legs and biscuit it in place.

The next step is to notch the back legs for the arms. Use the front legs as a guide. The notch is ¼" deep by the size of the arm's end. Mark and drill for dowels to attach the arms to the top of the front leg. Also drill clearance holes in the back legs to screw the rear of the arm to the back leg from the inside of the leg. With the bench still dry-assembled, lay out and drill ⅜" dowel holes for the slats.

After resolving any fitting problems, cut a ¼" × ¾" groove into the center of the bottom edge on the top rail. This will hold the slats' tenons. Then glue the bench together for real. Start by nailing the divider in place between the box front and back, holding the top edges flush. Then put glue on the biscuits and fit the legs onto the box parts, fitting the slats and top rail in place at the same time. There are a lot of pieces to align, but the glue will allow you about five minutes to check the slats before it starts to set.

The next step is to assemble and attach the seat frame. Biscuit the back and center pieces together, and then nail the frame in place to the assembled box. After all is dry, cut the radius on the top rail and leg ends. Rout a ¼" radius on all the edges of the top rail and smooth it out.

Breadboards & Lift Lids

The last step in assembling the bench is to make the lift lids with breadboard ends. These provide a seat and lid for the storage area below. Begin by gluing up two panels for the lids. Breadboards have been around for hundreds of years as a means of stabilizing a panel as it goes through humidity changes each season. Breadboards can be made in many ways that involve complicated joinery. I chose a method that is simple, and gives an authentic look. Rout three mortises in each breadboard 1" deep by 1½" long using the jig shown above. Use a chisel to square out the mortises. The breadboard ends are a little long, so cut them to length after attaching them to the panel with #10 × 3" pan-head screws. When you're happy with the fit of the breadboards, tap the fitted plugs in place with glue. Trim and sand the plugs flush. Attach the lids to the bench with continuous hinges.

Greene & Greene Hall Bench

LET.	NO.	ITEM	DIMENSIONS (INCHES)			MATERIAL
			T	W	L	
A	1	Top rail	¾	4⅝	45½	Cherry
B	2	Back legs*	2¾	4⅝	40	Cherry
C	2	Front legs	1¾	2⅛	23¾	Cherry
D	2	Large slats	⅝	4¼	18¼	Cherry
E	10	Small slats	⅝	2¼	18¼	Cherry
F	1	Center slat	⅝	1½	18¼	Cherry
G	2	Arms	1¾	2	20⅛	Cherry
H	2	Seat frame ends	¾	4¼	19	Cherry
I	1	Seat frame back*	¾	3½	41⅜	Cherry
J	1	Seat frame center	¾	2½	15½	Cherry
K	4	Breadboard ends**	¾	2½	15½	Cherry
L	2	Lids**	1¹⁄₁₆	15½	14⁷⁄₁₆	Cherry
M	2	Box ends	¾	8	16³⁄₁₆	Cherry
N	1	Box front	¾	8	46⅞	Cherry
O	1	Box back	¾	8	43⅝	Cherry
P	1	Divider	¾	7¼	17	Cherry
Q	1	Divider	¾	17½	48½	Plywood
		Plug material	⁵⁄₁₆	⁵⁄₁₆	30	Ebony
		Plug material	⁷⁄₁₆	⁷⁄₁₆	30	Ebony
	1	Continuous hinge		1½	48†	Antique-brass

*Rough length; **Requires fitting after assembly; †Cut in 19" lengths

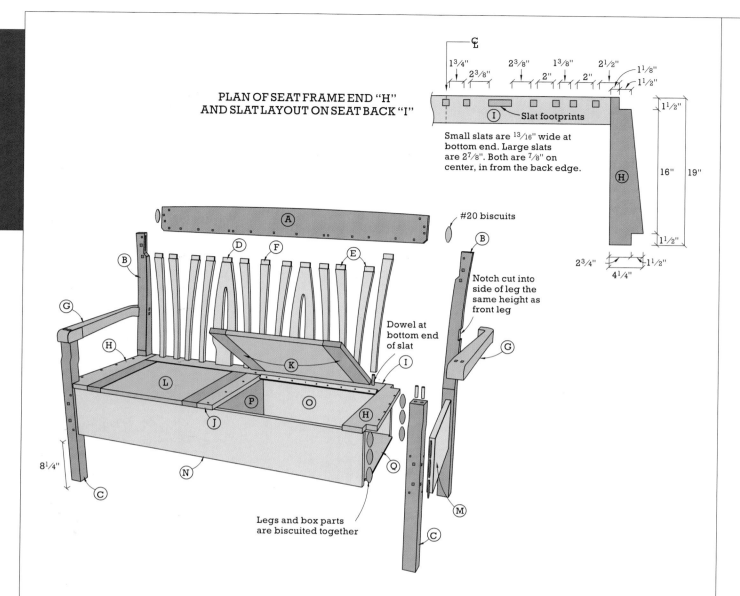

PLAN OF SEAT FRAME END "H" AND SLAT LAYOUT ON SEAT BACK "I"

$1^3/4$" $2^3/8$" $2^3/8$" $1^3/8$" $2^1/2$" $1^1/8$"
$2^3/8$" 2" 2" $1^1/2$"

Slat footprints

Small slats are $13/16$" wide at bottom end. Large slats are $2^7/8$". Both are $7/8$" on center, in from the back edge.

$1^1/2$"
16" 19"
$1^1/2$"

$2^3/4$" $1^1/2$"
$4^1/4$"

#20 biscuits

Notch cut into side of leg the same height as front leg

Dowel at bottom end of slat

Legs and box parts are biscuited together

$8^1/4$"

Planting the Plugs

The finishing accent for this piece, and one that is a trademark of the Greene & Greene style, is to add ebony plugs to many of the bench joints. See the next page for a handy way to do this. Adding color to this bench isn't terribly difficult. First, color the wood with J.E. Moser's Light Sheraton Mahogany water-soluble aniline dye (item #844-421, woodworker. com). Allow it to dry. Apply one coat of clear finish. Next, we used a brown glaze from Behlen's (item #916-759, wood-worker.com). Wipe the bench with your rag until most of it is colored evenly. Allow that to dry overnight. Then complete the process with two coats of a clear finish.

By the way, if you're wondering what a piece like this is worth these days, we sold this bench on eBay in 2000 for $1,200.

Cut the tenons on the seat, then cut the mortises in the breadboard ends. Now cut an elongated clearance hole at the bottom of the mortise. Screw the bread-boards in place and cap them with the rectangular plugs as shown.

Square Plugs & Square Holes Made Simple

There doesn't seem to be any rhyme or reason to the plug locations used by Greene and Greene, except that the plugs were symmetrical. Used ostensibly to hide screws, nails and other fasteners, there should be plugs at all of the major joint locations. There are two sizes of plugs, $5/16$" square and $7/16$" square. This is the fastest and easiest way to do this.

If there's a nail in the location of the plug, set it as deeply as you can.

Now drill a hole (either $3/8$" or $1/4$" in diameter) that's about $3/8$" deep.

Now square the hole. I bought inexpensive steel bar stock from a home center store ($7/16$" square and $5/16$" square). Then I tapered one end on my grinder. Tap the bar stock into your round hole and it will become a square hole.

Put a small dot of glue in the hole and tap your ebony plug in place.

Use a piece of cardboard as a spacer between your work and a flush-cutting saw. Cut the plug and then sand it slightly so there's still a raised bump.

Shaker Bench

BY JIM STUARD

With nothing more than wedged tenons and some good engineering, this is a phenomenally strong bench. The wedged tenons create a splayed dovetail effect that completely locks this bench together.

Begin construction by cutting out the four boards according to the Schedule of Materials. The extra length on the stretcher and legs is to accommodate a little extra length on the tenons for trimming.

After cutting and cleaning up the tenons, lay out and cut the through-mortises, which are angled to accommodate the wedged tenons. Cut the mortises to fit right over the tenons. To lay out the arc on the stretcher, drive a nail into the top of the arc at the center of the board. Then drive a nail into the starting point of both ends of the arc, as close to the edge of the board as possible. Take a strip of wood approximately $1/8" \times 1/2" \times 36"$ and bend it into an arc between the nails and trace a line on the stretcher. Remove the nails, cut out the arc and clean up the edge with a drawknife.

Now make the cutouts in the end panels. Lay them out according to the diagram, then cut them out with a coping saw. Make some relief cuts into the waste side to make cutting it out a little easier.

Once you have all the joinery fit, it's time to get ready to assemble the bench. This is a completely clamp-free glue up. The wedges driven into the tenons act as the "clamps" to hold the entire bench together. The wedges are cut at an angle wider than the 5° of the mortise because the wedge itself becomes compressed when driving into the tenon. This compression takes away some of the wedges' ability to spread the tenon. That's why you make wedges with a 7° taper. This yields a good spread on the tenon during assembly.

Now is the time to test a set of wedges in a joint. Using no glue, assemble a joint. Tap in a couple of wedges and see if they completely spread a joint apart before bottoming out in the tenon slot. If they leave a little room, cut a little off of the wedge's narrow end and taper it to fit the top of the slot accordingly. This gives a little more play to spread the tenon apart. Gently disassemble the dry-fit joint and proceed to glue up the bench

Taking some lumber from a friend's cherry tree, cut down, milled and air dried. I glued up two boards to make the top and ends for this bench. Some scraping of the joint is required after gluing. Try to arrange your boards so the joint between them is invisible.

Cut the tenons to the actual width on the table saw. Set the blade to 1" high, defining the length of the tenons. After marking the depth with a gauge, cut the waste out from between the tenons. Set the saw to $7/8"$ high for cutting the slots that accept the wedges used to hold the table together. See the diagram for the actual size of the outer parts of the tenon. Use a backing board on your miter gauge to hold the boards upright

and drive home the wedges with glue on them. It helps to wait a bit to clean up the squeezed-out glue. This lets it get a "skin" that keeps the mess to a minimum. Clean up with a chisel and a damp rag.

After cutting the tenon a little proud, mask off the tenon for sanding by taping around the entire tenon with two widths of masking tape. The tape keeps you from sanding a depression in the top

around the tenon. Chisel and plane an angle on all four sides of the tenons and round them over with a sander. Remove the tape and sand the rest of the bench to #150 grit. Apply three coats of clear finish and rub out your finish with some steel wool and wool wax, a lubricant you can find at many woodworking stores.

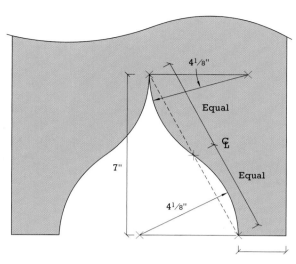

LEG CUTOUT

4¹⁄₈"
Equal
C̶L
7"
Equal
4¹⁄₈"

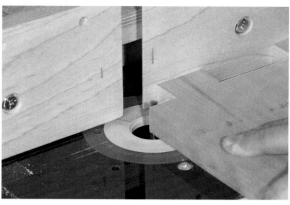

Next, set up the router table with a ¹⁄₄" straight bit to clean up the shoulders of the tenons. Mark on the router table fence where you need to stop and start each cut and gently push the tenon ends of the boards against the bit, missing the tenon.

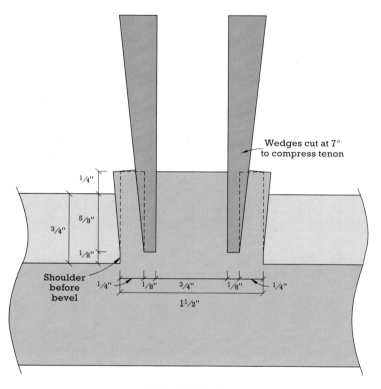

WEDGE DETAIL

Wedges cut at 7°
to compress tenon

¹⁄₄"
⁵⁄₈"
³⁄₄"
¹⁄₈"

Shoulder
before
bevel

¹⁄₄" ¹⁄₈" ³⁄₄" ¹⁄₈" ¹⁄₄"
1¹⁄₂"

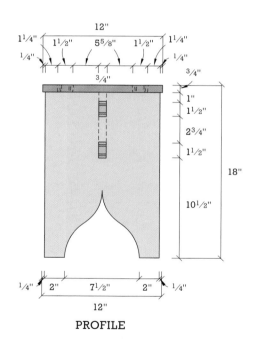

PROFILE

12"
1¹⁄₄" 1¹⁄₂" 5⁵⁄₈" 1¹⁄₂" 1¹⁄₄"
¹⁄₄" ¹⁄₄"
³⁄₄"
³⁄₄"
1"
1¹⁄₂"
2³⁄₄"
1¹⁄₂"
18"
10¹⁄₂"
¹⁄₄" 2" 7¹⁄₂" 2" ¹⁄₄"
12"

Shaker Bench

NO.	ITEM	DIMENSIONS (INCHES)			MATERIAL
		T	W	L	
1	Top	³⁄₄	12	36	Cherry
2	Ends*	³⁄₄	11¹⁄₂	18¹⁄₄	Cherry
1	Stretcher**	³⁄₄	6	28¹⁄₄	Cherry
16	Wedges	³⁄₄	¹⁄₂	3	Walnut

*¹⁄₄" added to length for trimming of tenon; **¹⁄₄" added to both ends for trimming of tenon

The wedges are cut on the table saw using a simple jig (see diagram below). The stock is $3/4" \times 6" \times 3"$. That means the grain direction is in the 3" dimension. Make a simple jig to hold the wedge stock while cutting on the saw.

When you can press fit everything together, make a simple angle gauge to cut the 5° angle on the narrow widths of the mortises. The 5° angle widens the top of the mortise by about $1/8"$. Split this measurement and mark both sides of the mortise, with a $1/16"$ offset, for setting the angle gauge. Before chiseling the angle, take a small saw and cut the sides of the mortises to the marks, reducing tearout. Clamp the gauge in place and gently chisel out the angle on the mortise sides. The angle shouldn't go completely to the other side of the mortise. This leaves a softer bend for the tenon to make (see diagram), thereby reducing cracking – something you have to be careful about in a brittle wood such as cherry.

When the glue is dry and cleaned up, make a template out of the cover from a steno pad. The front and back will do. Just tape them together and cut out a couple of holes for the tenons to come through. The more difficult set of tenons to reach are the ones below the top. Set your template up for those. Lay the template over the tenons and cut them flush with the template.

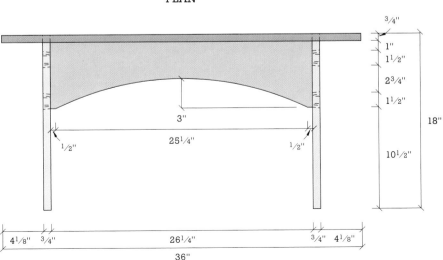

PLAN

$1/4"$
$1^1/4"$
$1^1/2"$
$2^5/8"$
$3/4"$
$2^5/8"$
$1^1/2"$
$1^1/4"$
$1/4"$
12"

$4^1/8"$ $3/4"$ $26^1/4"$ $3/4"$ $4^1/8"$
36"

ELEVATION

$3/4"$
1"
$1^1/2"$
$2^3/4"$
$1^1/2"$
18"
$10^1/2"$

3"
$25^1/4"$
$1/2"$ $1/2"$

$4^1/8"$ $3/4"$ $26^1/4"$ $3/4"$ $4^1/8"$
36"

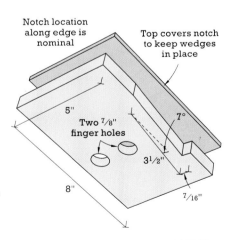

Notch location along edge is nominal

Top covers notch to keep wedges in place

5"

Two $7/8"$ finger holes

7°

$3^1/2"$

8"

$7/16"$

WEDGE-CUTTING JIG, SHOWN FROM BELOW

Japanese Garden Bench

BY CHRISTOPHER SCHWARZ & KARA GEBHART UHL

We used a miter saw to cut our pieces to length. Here you can see that we clamped all the top boards together and "gang cut" them to length simultaneously.

My father always has had a knack for doing more with less. He built the first house on our farm using a Skil saw, a drill and a hammer.

Sometime during my childhood he built a pair of these Japanese-looking benches using leftover 2×4s and framing nails. While visiting him one recent summer, I was struck by the fact that they have survived more than a dozen winters and still look good.

This project is really great for the beginning woodworker who doesn't have a lot of tools, skills or confidence. But the end result will make you look like you've got all three, in spades.

Trip to the Lumberyard
This bench is designed to be built using just five 10'-long 2×4s. You can build it from sugar pine, paint it and spend less than $20. I always liked redwood for my outdoor projects (and that's what the originals were made from) so I spent the extra cash – about $200.

No matter what species you pick, select the straightest, most knot-free 2×4s you can find. While you're at the lumberyard, pick up a pound of stainless-steel screws. Former *Popular Woodworking* managing editor Kara Gebhart Uhl (who helped me build this project) and I used #8 × 2" screws. Another sound choice would be Miller Dowels (millerdowel.com).

Back in the Shop
You don't need a jointer, planer or table saw to build this bench. You don't even need a shop. A drill, a saw, some sandpaper and a couple of sawhorses will get the job done right on your driveway.

Start by laying out your crosscuts on the 2×4s using chalk. Pick the best-looking boards for the five top pieces. Boards with too many knots or dings can be used as legs, which are mostly covered up by the top pieces.

Then cut all your pieces to length as shown in the cutting list on page 22.

What's important to remember here is that it's not critical if you cut your legs a bit long or cut the top boards a bit short. What is important is that you cut all the legs the same length, whatever that turns out to be. For that reason, I recommend "gang cutting" your parts.

"Gang cutting" is when you clamp together all the parts that are the same length and trim them to size simultaneously, as shown above. This works no matter what tool you use for crosscutting.

Sanding (Insert Groan Here)
It's tempting to screw this project together immediately, but I'd suggest you do all you can to resist the urge to assemble.

A better bet is for you to sand all your pieces to remove marks and dings. This helps get them ready for whatever finish you'll be applying (paint, deck stain, tung oil or nothing).

Once the faces and edges have been sanded, you need to "break the edges" of all the boards. This is pretty simple to do. Just grab some #120-grit sandpaper and take a couple of licks on all the edges of each board (you're trying to remove any sharp edges). This will make the bench more comfortable to sit on and less likely to splinter when it gets wet.

Leg Assembly
This bench goes together quickly. Chuck a bit in your drill to give you a $^3/_{16}$" pilot hole and a countersink simultaneously.

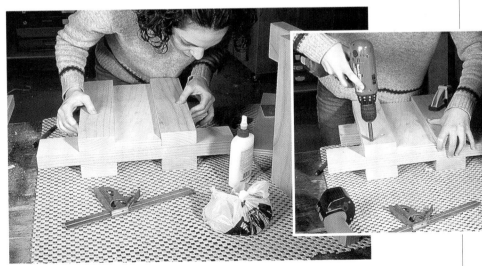

Use scraps as spacers to ensure that your leg assemblies go together just right. This is a lot easier than measuring everything. Then screw it together using stainless steel screws.

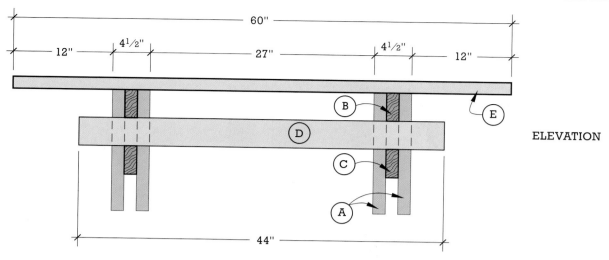

ELEVATION

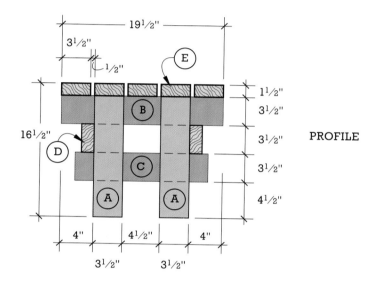

PROFILE

These bits are available from most home-supply or hardware stores.

Begin by assembling one of the leg structures. First find a piece of scrap that's 4¹⁄₂" wide and place it between two of the leg pieces.

Center the top cross brace on the two legs, flush everything up, then glue and screw the cross brace to the legs using two screws in each. You can use polyurethane glue or a water-resistant glue such as Titebond II.

Put another piece of scrap 2×4 against the top cross brace and center the low cross brace below that scrap. Then glue and screw the low cross brace to the legs.

Next, put two more legs on top of the cross braces and place the 4¹⁄₂" scrap spacer between them. Glue and screw these two legs to the cross braces. Repeat this same procedure for the other leg assembly. You're almost done.

Plug It Up

For a finished look, we took a few minutes to plug the holes made by the countersink. Our countersink made a ³⁄₈"-diameter hole.

You can plug the hole with store-bought ³⁄₈" plugs or ³⁄₈"-diameter dowels. We took some ³⁄₈" × ³⁄₈" square stock,

whittled one end and glued it in place. The square corners of the wood cut the round hole into a square one. Once your plugs are glued in place, cut or sand them flush.

Final Assembly

Stand the legs upright on your work surface and put the stretchers in place between the two cross braces. Glue and screw the stretchers into place and plug the holes left by the countersink.

Then arrange the five top boards on the base. Because the pith side of flat-grained wood is more prone to raised grain, make sure you place all your boards bark-side up. (Look at the growth rings.)

To ensure everything was spaced evenly, we first attached the top pieces at the front and back of the bench using glue and screws. Then we centered the middle board between those. Finally, we put the remaining two boards in place and figured out what gap should be between each board. We then glued and screwed these two boards in place. Finally, we plugged the holes.

Check out Bob Flexner's advice on protecting exterior wood on the next page. We chose to leave the wood in its natural state and allow it to turn a silvery-gray, which will happen when left outside.

Japanese Garden Bench

LET.	NO.	ITEM	DIMENSIONS (INCHES)			MATERIAL
			T	W	L	
A	8	Legs	1¹⁄₂	3¹⁄₂	15	Redwood
B	2	Top cross braces	1¹⁄₂	3¹⁄₂	19¹⁄₂	Redwood
C	2	Low cross braces	1¹⁄₂	3¹⁄₂	16	Redwood
D	2	Stretchers	1¹⁄₂	3¹⁄₂	44	Redwood
E	5	Top boards	1¹⁄₂	3¹⁄₂	60	Redwood

Protecting Exterior Wood

There is probably more misunderstanding about how to protect wood outdoors than about any other aspect of wood finishing.

The need for a quality coating to protect exterior wood is great because when sunlight or water come into frequent contact with wood, the wood can lose its color, split, warp and often rot.

The best way to protect exposed wood is to apply a paint or finish that blocks sunlight and moisture, and holds up to these elements.

• **Light** is the principal enemy of paints and finishes. Over time, ultraviolet rays, which are strongest from direct sunlight, break down paints. If you catch it before the paint is damaged all the way through, you can rub off the dull, chalky result with abrasives (contained in many car polishes, for example) and expose paint that looks shiny and new.

UV rays also break down clear finishes, but most of the damage here will come when they peel. The finish peels because the UV rays penetrate the film and destroy the lignin that holds the cellulose cells of wood fiber together. The surface cells separate and the finish bonded to these cells peels.

The best sun-blocking agents are pigments (contained in paints and stains). But pigments hide the wood, and many people would rather have it visible. Other good sun-blocking agents are UV absorbers, which are similar to sunscreen agents used in suntan lotions. They convert UV light energy to heat energy, which dissipates. UV absorbers don't hide wood, and they are effective at preventing deterioration, but they are expensive, and a significant amount (1 percent to 3 percent by weight) has to be in the finish to be effective.

• **Moisture** also causes paints and finishes to peel when it gets between the coating and the wood. Paints resist moisture penetration well, but most clear finishes don't. Water repellents, which contain a low-surface-tension waxy substance, cause water to bead but water repellents don't totally keep moisture out of the wood.

The best moisture-resistant clear finishes are varnishes called spar or marine varnish that are made to be very flexible so they can keep up with extreme wood movement. Varnishes made with phenolic resin and tung oil are best because they don't crack as quickly as those made with polyurethane resin.

The best way to protect wood outdoors is to paint it. Paint repels water and blocks UV rays effectively. There are two major categories of paint: oil-based and water-based (also called latex).

Oil-based paints are best for objects such as chairs and picnic tables because latex paints don't wear as well. Oil-based primer also is best on wood that has been exposed to the weather for a month or more because it penetrates deeper than latex primers. If the wood is freshly milled or sanded, acrylic-latex primers perform well.

Water-based or latex paints offer the best protection for wood siding because they allow moisture vapor to pass through better than oil-based paints. If the water vapor can't get through the paint and to the outside environment, it will build up behind the paint and cause it to peel. A primer coat of oil-based paint is not thick enough to stop the penetration of moisture.

No clear finishes work as well as paint if they are exposed to bright light, but expensive marine varnishes come closest. Keep in mind, however, that these finishes are very glossy and relatively soft (for flexibility), and you need to apply eight or nine coats to reach maximum UV resistance.

– Bob Flexner, contributing editor

Left unfinished, white oak and other weather-resistant woods will turn a silvery-gray. This Adirondack chair has survived 10 seasons outside with little deterioration.

Stickley Ottoman

BY DAVID THIEL

A Morris chair (heck, almost any chair) just isn't complete without an ottoman to prop your feet on. Sadly, by the time you finish building the chair you're usually so glad to have completed the project that the ottoman gets delayed until later. Well, now is the time!

Over the years we've published a number of plans for Morris chairs in *Popular Woodworking* in varying styles and by several designers. After looking at dozens of comparable ottomans, we selected a traditional and simple design from Gustav Stickley.

The No. 300 ottoman we used as a model is one of Stickley's earlier pieces. Originally offered with a hard leather seat, it sold for $7.50 in the 1912 catalog. Recent auctions have seen this simple piece sell for as much as $800. The dimensions on our project match Stickley's, but we've updated the seat material to adjust the cost (as well as to make it a little more comfortable).

How to Build It

As far as furniture projects go, this one is basic. But it does give you a chance to work on a hallmark joint of Arts & Crafts furniture – the mortise and tenon.

There are four mortises per leg, but for the first-time builder the construction method used is very forgiving. The blind tenons, including the ones in the top rail joints (which ultimately are hidden by the upholstery) are easy.

The simplicity of the mortise-and-tenon joint is spruced up a little on this piece with the addition of pegs, which make the joints more solid and add a nice decorative touch.

The more significant step only sharp-eyed woodworkers will notice at first is to make the legs from multiple pieces of wood. By doing so, the highly figured quartersawn white oak shows on all four sides. Mother Nature hasn't figured out how to do this yet, but we have.

Also, if upholstery is something that has kept you from trying this type of project before, don't sweat it. I'm hardly an upholsterer myself, and everyone who has seen my ottoman seems to think it turned out pretty well, so we've included a short sidebar about the upholstery (see "Upholstery Made Easy" on page 28).

Four-faced Legs

Quartersawn white oak is one of the features that dresses up the plain styling of Arts & Crafts furniture. Cut from the center of the log out to the bark, the orientation of the growth rings runs almost perfectly perpendicular to the face of the board. This reveals splashes of "ray flake" that are beautiful to behold, but they only happen on the perpendicular faces.

There are a few good ways to give the legs this ray flake on all four faces, but Stickley chose to simply add quartersawn veneer to the two flat-sawn faces, which I copied.

Start making the legs by cutting eight leg halves that are $7/8" \times 2" \times 16"$. The $7/8"$ thickness will require you to start with 4/4 rough lumber, but ultimately the oversized dimensions will be to your benefit, as you'll see.

First, glue each of the four leg pairs together, face-to-face, orienting the best quartersawn grain pattern to the outside. When the glue has dried, square one corner of each piece on the jointer, then size each leg (using your table saw, then your jointer for a final pass) to $1\frac{5}{8}"$ (across the face that shows a seam) $\times 1\frac{3}{8}"$ or slightly larger (across the quartersawn face).

These dimensions will allow you to add $\frac{1}{8}"$-thick veneer to the two layered faces, then run the entire leg down to $1\frac{1}{2}"$ square, leaving an almost invisible veneer face on two sides.

Next, run eight veneer pieces to $\frac{1}{8}"$ $\times 1\frac{3}{4}" \times 16"$. If $\frac{1}{8}"$ is thinner than you're comfortable running on your planer, leave it at $\frac{1}{4}"$ – just know that you'll have to plane more off those faces after glue-up. Glue the veneer pieces to the leg blanks, making sure the veneer extends over all the edges.

After the glue has dried, trim the veneer pieces flush to the leg centers (I used a No. 3 handplane). Then run the veneer faces through the planer (alternating sides on each pass) until the leg is $1\frac{1}{2}"$ square. Trim the legs to length for a four-faced leg.

Making the Holes

The next step is to find where you want the mortises to be on the legs. First determine the orientation of the legs (best faces out), then use the illustrations above to mark the mortise locations.

The mortises can be $\frac{3}{8}"$ wide, and that's fine, but to be honest with you, I had a $\frac{1}{2}"$ mortise chisel in my mortiser, so that's where they ended up. I cut the mortises $1\frac{1}{16}"$ deep to allow an extra $\frac{1}{16}"$ for glue squeeze-out. Cut the mortises, then be sure to clean the chips out of the bottoms so the tenons will seat properly.

Filling the Holes

I cut my tenons on the table saw with a single combination blade. If you have a dado stack on hand, use it.

If you opt for "one-piece" legs without adding veneer, choose the best grain pattern to face "forward." Take a close look at the grain on the pieces for your legs and mark the tops to offer the best look.

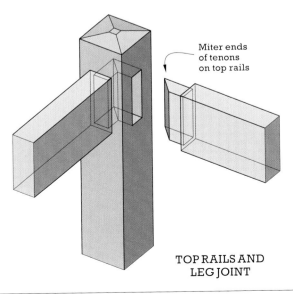

Miter ends of tenons on top rails

TOP RAILS AND LEG JOINT

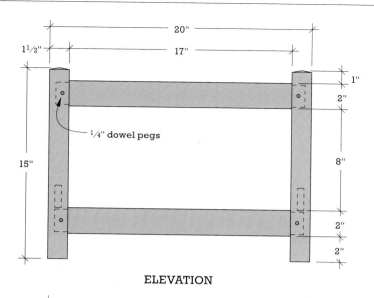

ELEVATION

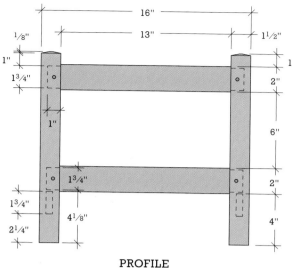

PROFILE

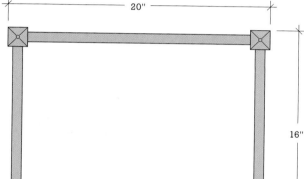

PLAN

A dado stack will allow you to cut your tenons faster. Because my mortises are ½" wide, all of the shoulders on my tenons are ⅛". This makes it unnecessary to change the blade height when moving from face to edge shoulders.

Because the top rails are all at the same height on the legs, the tenons will bump into each other before fully seating against the leg. Take a minute to miter the ends of the tenons on the top rails so they can meet without interfering with the fit. Because the lower rails are staggered in height, this isn't a problem.

With all the tenons cut, test-fit the ottoman. Assemble both ends, then insert the longer rails between the two assemblies. The tenons should require a little wiggling to slip all the way into the mortises, but you shouldn't have to bang on them with a hammer. Check to be sure that all the shoulders fit flush against the legs without any gaps. When all the joints are acceptable, go ahead and disassemble the frame.

Topping the Legs

When laying out the mortise locations on the legs, you will probably notice that the top rails will sit 1" short of the tops of the legs. Don't freak out – you didn't do anything wrong. This extra space leaves room for the upholstery material and space for you to bevel the tops to dress them up a little.

Grab a combination square or other similar tool that will help you mark a line ⅛" down from the top of the leg on all four faces. Then set your disc sander's table to a 12° angle and, using a miter gauge on the sander, slowly bevel the tops of the legs on all four sides. This will leave a ¼" × ¼" square at the top. This bevel is a great detail.

Stickley Ottoman

LET.	NO.	ITEM	DIMENSIONS (INCHES)			MATERIAL	COMMENTS
			T	W	L		
A	4	Legs	1½	1½	15	White oak	*
B	2	Lower rails	¾	2	19	White oak	1" TBE
C	2	Lower rails	¾	2	15	White oak	1" TBE
D	2	Top rails	¾	2	19	Poplar	1" TBE, mitered
E	2	Top rails	¾	2	15	Poplar	1" TBE, mitered

*For solid legs. For build-up dimensions, see page 25; TBE = tenons, both ends

Steel Edge or Mineral Grit?

Now is the appropriate time to smooth the wood to the surface finish that you prefer. While we'll often just tell you to sand using #100 to #220 grits, there is another option here.

Because of the possible dramatic effect of the grain in the quartersawn white oak, preparing the wood to best present the grain is key. When you sand wood you effectively tear the ends of the fibers to smooth the wood surface. This leaves a feathery end to the grain structure and can obscure the grain pattern and affect the way the wood takes a stain.

A better method for this project is to cut the ends of the fibers using a hand scraper or scraper plane. With a little extra effort (and a lot less dust) you can leave crisp ends on the fibers that will really let the ray flake pop when you add the finish.

Supplies

Woodworker's Supply
woodworker.com or 800-645-9292

4 oz. • J.E. Moser's Golden Amber Maple water-soluble aniline dye, item #844-750, $27.49

1 qt. • Behlen's Van Dyke Shading & Glazing Stain, item #916-759, $28.99

Prices as of publication date.

Ready for Assembly

With all the pieces test-fit and sanded (or scraped), you're ready to put the ottoman together.

Jut as with the test run, assemble the ends first, applying glue to the inside of the mortises, lightly covering all four walls. Applying the glue to the mortise rather than the tenon will keep glue squeeze-out (and clean up) to a minimum. With the ends assembled

and clamped, go ahead and insert the long rails and clamp them as well. You're nearly done.

A Bunch of Pegs

The last detail before finishing is to peg all the tenons. I use ¼" red oak dowel stock for this step. You can use white oak, but the white oak dowels are harder to find at the store, and the red oak makes the pegs stand out a bit more on the leg once color is applied.

Chuck a ¼"-diameter bit into your drill and use a drill stop collar or a piece of tape to make the 1" depth necessary to drill through the tenon and into the opposite wall of the mortise.

Mark all the peg locations, then start drilling. You can peg the holes as you go (add the glue to the hole, not the peg) or wait until all the holes are drilled before gluing.

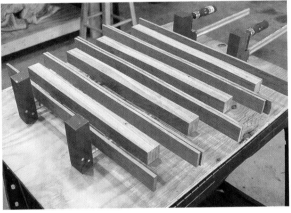

To offer four faces with quartersawn white oak on each leg, the leg centers are glued then planed to 1⅝" × 1⅜". Then the ⅛" or ¼" oversize "skins" of quartersawn veneer are glued to the flat-sawn faces. After the glue dries, plane the legs to their finished 1½" × 1½" dimension.

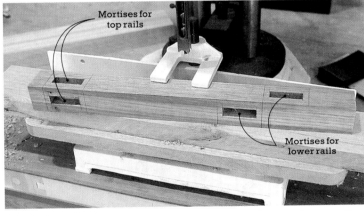

The mortises for the top rails are on adjacent inside faces and intersect in the middle of the leg. The mortises for the lower rails are staggered to fit one on top of the other. I used a bench-top hollow-chisel mortiser to make quick work of the mortises, but a router (or even a chisel and mallet) will work just as well.

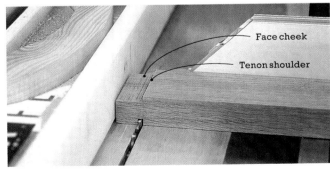

The shoulders for all the rail tenons are made with little fuss on the table saw. Define the shoulder on the first pass using a miter gauge for support, then nibble the rest of the material away, backing the piece away from the rip fence.

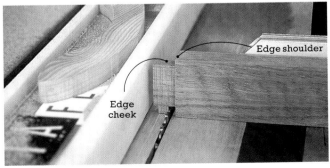

Cut the adjacent shoulders and cheeks in the same manner. I'm using a combination blade here, which leaves a corduroy-like finish on the cheeks. Because of that, I've left the tenons oversized and will use a shoulder plane to pare them to fit.

One of the most visible details on the ottoman is the shallow bevel on the leg tops. You could make the cuts using a table saw or miter saw, but I took advantage of a bench-top disc sander that let me fine-tune the bevels as I went.

Cut all the pegs ¼" longer than the depth of your holes. Then, when the peg is fully seated in the hole, trim the excess with a flush-cut saw with little or no set to the teeth. If you don't have such a saw, slide a piece of cardboard under the blade to keep from scratching the face of the leg. Do a little more sanding or scraping around the pegs and you're ready to break out the dye.

Color Me Nutty Brown

As mentioned, quartersawn white oak can be amazing to look at, but a finish designed to enhance the wood helps a lot.

I use a water-based aniline dye to put the first layer of color on the wood. Because the dye is water-based, it will raise the grain when applied. So to prepare the wood for finishing, I first wipe down the entire piece with a damp cloth (just water) then hand-sand the piece with #220-grit paper to knock off the burrs.

Next, add the aniline dye and let it dry overnight. Then it's time for a coat of brown glaze. The glaze is a stain, but it's the consistency of thin pudding and will lay on the wood and fill the grain slightly. Let the color infuse the grain, but be sure to wipe off the excess or it will hide the wood.

Let the glaze dry overnight again, then you're ready for your favorite clear, protective top coat. With a project this size, I often use lacquer in a spray can with good results. The rest is upholstery. Use the sidebar on the next page to help you through these steps.

Then you're ready to put your feet up and relax.

Start by mitering the corners of the muslin around the legs and tacking the edges to the inside of the rails, tightening the material as you go.

Cut out the corners of the batting sheet and wrap it around the legs and rails, tightening as you go. Tack the batting to the inside of the rails.

A layer of 2" foam will add cushion. The piece should be cut to fit just inside the rails and will lay in place on the first batting layer.

A second layer of batting holds the foam in place. It is cut and attached exactly as the first layer, but keep tightening the material to maintain a uniform look.

Upholstery Made Easy

If you've been waiting to tackle a first upholstery project, this is a simple one. All you need are a few yards of black muslin (or similar material), some foam block, batting and a finished cover of your choice. You can find all the materials you need to upholster furniture at your local craft-supply store or fabric store.

As you can see, I used my pneumatic stapler (a wide-crown is great if you have one, but narrow-crown will work in a pinch), but you can use standard upholstery tacks as well. The photos walk you through all the steps except the finished cover, which is the same process as used in attaching the last batting layer (shown in the top right photo).

A top layer of muslin covers the batting and foam. The corners are miter-cut, then folded around the legs to avoid loose strings and unraveling.

The final muslin layer is tucked around the rail and tacked at the center. Then work out toward the legs, rolling and tacking as necessary. Trim any excess.

Shaker-Inspired Bench

BY ROBERT W. LANG

There is an old Shaker hymn called "Simple Gifts" that begins with this line: "Tis the gift to be simple." This bench carries many of the qualities that the Shakers valued. The design is straightforward and driven by function, yet it's also graceful and elegant. The construction is obvious and building it doesn't require anything beyond simple tools and techniques.

The antique Shaker bench that inspired this piece actually led two lives. It was originally made without a back at the Hancock Shaker village. As it got older (and presumably the brothers or sisters using it also got older), wood was scabbed onto the back of the ends, and the backrest was added, making it more comfortable.

Made of pine, the original was longer – 94" – and likely was used with a dining table. I liked the look and simplicity of this piece, but I decided to make a shorter version for use in an entry hall or mudroom.

I used cherry, and happened upon a single board that was wide enough, and long enough, for the seat and the end pieces. If you're not as fortunate, you'll need to glue up stock for width, which is what I was planning to do on the way to the lumberyard.

Adapting the Design

The original seat was 1" thick, and the corbel supports were short pieces at each end. Because I would be using ¾"-thick materials, I extended the seat supports to run all the way between the ends to brace the seat and strengthen the overall structure.

The second design change was to the ends – on the original the arched cutout that creates the legs of the bench wasn't centered on the end. Because the back was added, the cutout was pushed forward. I put the cutout at the mid-point of the ends and made it taller and elliptical.

Easy Layout, Strong Joinery

I stayed with the simple joinery of my example; a dado in the bottom of the seat to capture the ends and two more in the back rail to capture the back supports. Lap joints where the seat supports meet the ends complete the joinery.

After all the parts were cut to size, I routed the ¾"-wide × ¼"-deep dados in the bottom of the seat, and the back of the back rail. I made the T-square jig as shown at left to guide the router, and to locate all of the joints the same distance in from the ends.

With the dados cut, I made a test assembly of the two ends and the seat. When I prepared the stock, I planed everything to just more than ¾". I made some final adjustments to the thickness of the ends with a hand plane to get a nice snug fit in the dados.

With these three pieces fit together, I turned them upside down on my bench. After making sure that the ends were square to the seat, I marked the seat supports' locations working from the ends, as shown below left.

While I managed to avoid having to measure for the locations of the lap joints on the stretcher, I did need to measure for the depth of the cuts. Because the ends recess into the ¼" dado in the seat, the lap joint cuts need to be ⅛" deeper than half the width of the support rails. The cuts in the rails and ends were marked at 1⅞" using the end of my adjustable square.

Guiding Hand Tools

Like the dados in the seat, there are numerous ways to cut the lap joints. The

This T-square jig locates the exact position of the router bit. The addition of an end stop on the bottom of the jig puts the cuts the same distance from the ends of both the seat and the back rail.

With the ends placed in the dados in the bottom of the seat, you can mark the location of the lap-joint cuts in the seat rail without measuring.

End stop

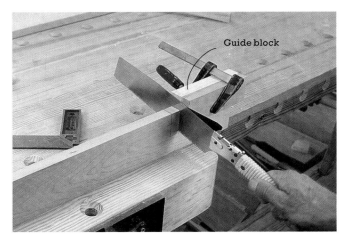

Clamp the guide block for the saw to just cover the pencil lines. By pressing the saw to the block as the cut is started, you establish a straight kerf.

After the bottom of the joint has been cut, use the same guide block to guide the chisel to pare the sides of the joint.

seat supports are rather long, so I decided not to risk using the table saw, but cut them with a Japanese handsaw and guide block as shown above. With the guide block clamped on the edge of my layout lines, it was easy to keep the saw straight, and I had the long cuts made quickly.

I used a jigsaw to make the bottom cuts, but I could just as easily have used a coping saw. I used the same guide block to pare the sides of the joints with a chisel, as shown above. I also used a rasp to fine-tune the fit. These joints are relatively easy to make, but you need to be careful – if you try to force them together, there is a good chance that the pieces could split, especially with cherry.

I like to sneak up on a good fit by testing the slots next to the adjacent slot rather than in them. If the wood should split, don't despair. You can usually glue the split pieces back together without losing any strength, or the repair ever being visible.

With the lap joints complete, I turned to the back supports. By making them as separate pieces, cutting the back taper

is very simple. I used my band saw and started the taper $1/4$" above the intersection with the seat, tapering to $1^3/4$" at the top of the support. After making the cuts, remove the saw marks by running the pieces over the jointer, then cut the radius at the top of the ends with a jigsaw or coping saw.

To make the ends a single piece, I simply glued the back supports to the ends. I used a butt joint, and had to be careful while clamping this up to keep everything aligned. You might want to add some biscuits to help keep the pieces in the same plane. Once the glue was dry, I cleaned up the joints with a card scraper, and I was then ready to cut the decorative curves.

I made a full-size pattern of the cutout in the ends, and the corbel at the end of the seat supports. I transferred the patterns to the pieces and then made the cuts with a jigsaw. I cleaned up the cuts by sanding the curves with an oscillating spindle sander. Again, there are many ways to make these cuts and smooth the surfaces. A band saw or coping saw could

have made the cuts, and the curves could be smoothed with a spokeshave, a card scraper or a sanding block.

Edges With Character

I prefer to ease the sharp edges on a piece like this by hand with a block plane, and I did most of this before assembling the bench, being careful to avoid the areas in the vicinity of the joints. I could have used a router with a roundover or chamfer bit, but I enjoy the process of doing it by hand, and I like to vary the radius in different areas, adding character to the piece. With a router, I would have ended up with a sterile sameness on every edge.

The edges on the inside curves of the end cutouts were shaped with a spokeshave as shown on page 33. After everything was put together, the edges near the joints were eased with a knife, a skew chisel and a rasp.

I did most of the sanding before assembly, sanding to #150 grit by hand with a sanding block. I avoided sanding in the areas of the joints to keep the joints from becoming sloppy. While

Shaker-Inspired Bench

NO.	ITEM	DIMENSIONS (INCHES)			MATERIAL	COMMENTS
		T	W	L		
2	Ends	$3/4$	$12^3/4$	$17^1/2$	Cherry	
2	Back supports	$3/4$	$2^7/8$	30	Cherry	Glue to ends after joints are cut
1	Back rail	$3/4$	$3^1/2$	54	Cherry	
2	Seat supports	$3/4$	$3^1/2$	53	Cherry	
1	Seat	$3/4$	$12^3/4$	54	Cherry	

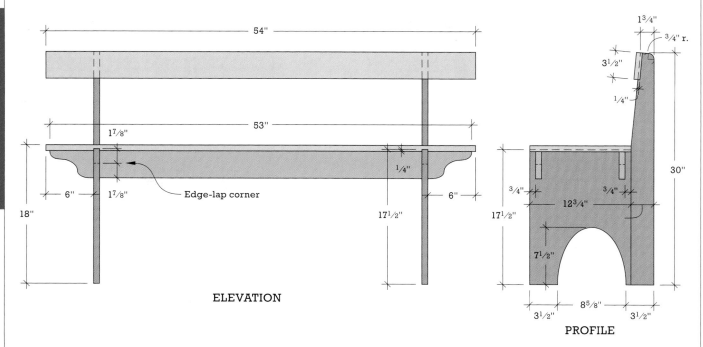

ELEVATION

PROFILE

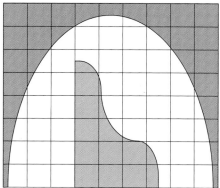

QUARTER-SIZE PATTERNS
Each square = 1"

hand sanding can be tedious, it leaves a much better surface, particularly on narrow edges, than using a random-orbit or palm sander.

Because the lap joints have a good deal of mechanical strength, I didn't need to clamp them together. I did clamp a "speed square" in the corners to keep things from racking while the glue dried. After an hour, I put glue on the top of the end pieces, and the top of the support rails. Then I clamped the seat and back, and left the assembly overnight for the glue to dry.

A Bit of Insurance

In the photo of the original Shaker bench, the ends of the dowels or plugs are visible on the face of the back rail and on the front edges of the joints for the seat supports. I decided to reinforce these joints, as well as the dado in the seat, with #8 × 1¾" screws, covering the screw heads with contrasting plugs of black walnut.

Years ago I did repair work on wooden boats, and plugged screws were the way we held nearly everything together. Here are a couple of tricks from those days that speed the process considerably.

Most people cut plugs in a random pattern in a piece of scrap and then pry them out with a chisel. If you rip the scrap to roughly the outside diameter of the plug cutter, and use a fence on the

After the joints are cut and the back extension is glued on, position the paper pattern and mark the arched cutout.

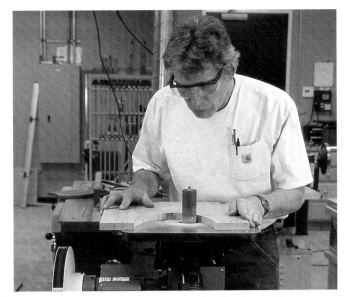

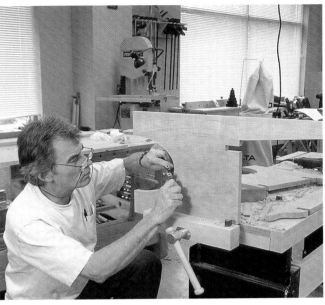

The oscillating spindle sander is ideal for cleaning up the saw marks and sanding to the inside of the pencil line.

A spokeshave eases the edges the block plane couldn't reach.

drill press as shown on the next page, the plug cutter won't need to remove so much material, and it won't tend to wander.

The second benefit is that the plugs don't need to be pried loose with a chisel. Set the blade height on the table saw to ⅛" less than the strip of plugs, and set the fence so that the plugs are on the outside of the blade. Use a push stick to carefully make the cut, and you have a strip with the plugs still attached. You can easily break them off when you're ready to use them, as shown on the next page.

Flush-cutting handsaws can be used for trimming the plugs, but I prefer to use a chisel. Pay attention to which way the grain is running on the side of the plug, and make the cut with the edge of the chisel on the "downhill" side. I hold the chisel slightly above the surface, and one smack with a mallet removes most of the plug. A paring cut, pushed by hand, leaves the plug flush with the surface.

If I'm not sure which way the plug will break, I'll make the first cut higher up, so that the plug is entirely above the surface, and then make the final cut in the direction that the first cut broke. This technique is faster than sawing, and a minimal amount of work with a scraper leaves the plug smooth and flush with the surface, as there are no saw marks to be sanded out.

A Fitting Finish

With the entire piece assembled, it was time to finish the work on the edges of the bench and to give it all a final sanding. I sanded all of the edges with #120-grit sandpaper, followed by #150. With the majority of the flat surfaces sanded to #150 grit before assembly, only minor sanding was needed before the entire piece was hand sanded with #240 grit.

Cherry is truly a beautiful wood, and it's my opinion that an oil finish brings out the best of its character and figure. I used a Danish oil finish, and wiped it on, working in the oil with a nylon abrasive pad, and keeping the surface wet for about 45 minutes.

After wiping the surface dry with a rag, I set the bench in the sun for a few hours, turning it every half hour and

The lap joints should slide together with hand pressure and don't need to be clamped together. Speed squares clamped in the corners keep the assembly from racking while the glue dries.

wiping off any oil that bled out. This exposure to the sun darkened the wood, giving a jump start to the patina that cherry develops as it ages.

The next morning I applied a second coat of oil, keeping the surface wet for 20 minutes before wiping it dry. I let the oil dry during a long weekend, and applied two coats of paste wax, worked in with a nylon pad and then buffed.

We tend to think that the furniture we sit on needs to be intricate in design and complicated to build. This Shaker bench proves otherwise.

Spend a little time preparing stock for plugs, and they will be easier to cut. The rabbet in the fence keeps chips from building up.

Keeping the plugs barely attached to the strip keeps them manageable. Break them off from the strip by hand.

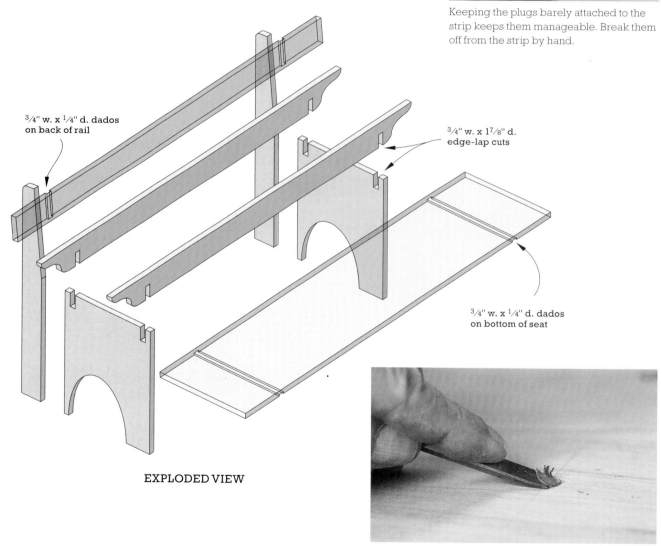

$3/4$" w. x $1/4$" d. dados on back of rail

$3/4$" w. x $1^7/8$" d. edge-lap cuts

$3/4$" w. x $1/4$" d. dados on bottom of seat

EXPLODED VIEW

It's faster to trim the plugs with a chisel than with a saw, and if you keep an eye on the grain direction they will be flush with the surface.

Jatoba Bench

BY BERT JOHANSEN

My lovely wife asked me to build a bench for our entry hall. After considering the intended space – which consists of an 11' wall – I initially planned on an 8' bench and sketched several possible options. However, the more I considered the challenges of building such a long bench and crafting the joinery so that the bench wouldn't warp, I opted for two 4' benches instead. And although they are intended for indoor use, I decided to make them suitable for outside as well, because the final design is perfect for a garden bench and who knows what the grandkids will do when they inherit them?

Influenced by Japanese design and inspired by its versatility, I crafted this simple bench using hidden stainless steel hardware for durability in either indoor or outdoor settings. For materi-als I selected jatoba with ebony accents. Dimensions of the completed project are 48" × 19 1/4" × 14".

Procure the wood and hardware, then joint and surface-plane the stock to final thickness.

Lay out the parts and make the straight cuts on the table saw. Cut the legs and rails to final length, but leave the slats and stretcher an inch or two longer than the final dimension. It is a good idea to make an extra slat and an extra leg as you proceed, as tearout when you machine the curved edges could be a problem.

Making the Bench Top

The top consists of nine slats and 16 ebony spacers, held together by two stainless-steel all-thread rods. Draw a fair curve for the top of the slats and cre-

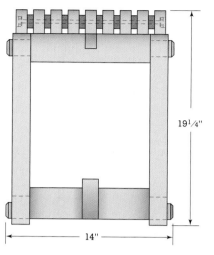

PROFILE

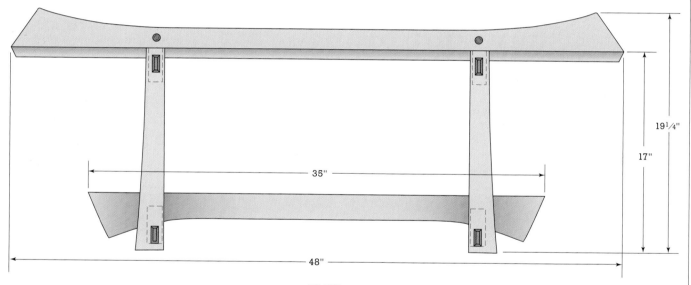

PLAN

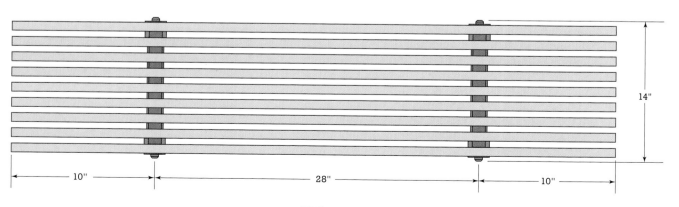

ELEVATION

ate a template from $\frac{1}{2}$" plywood. Sand the curved top edge smooth. (An oscillating spindle sander expedites this job – and many others in this project.) Drill $\frac{5}{16}$" holes exactly 10" from the ends of the template, as shown on the drawing on page 38. Use the template to trace the curved profile and cut the slats on your band saw, leaving about $\frac{1}{16}$" outside the line. (Don't cut them to final length yet.)

Attach the template to each slat with double-stick tape and use a pattern-routing bit at the router table to clean up the band saw cuts. Be aware of the grain direction, as jatoba is brittle and can easily tear out during edge treatment. You may have to climb cut as you rout the rising edge.

Remove the template and cut the ends to final size using your miter saw set to 30°. Carefully sand the curved slats on the oscillating spindle sander, or with a sanding drum on your drill press. These surfaces are the most important aspect of the project, as they constitute the bench seat. Users will invariably caress the surface with their fingers, and you want to eliminate any "ripple" from the router bit – hence the importance of the sanding.

The center "keel" slat has an extra inch added to the bottom. As you will see, this allows the use of a bridle joint to attach the top to the top rails. As shown on the drawing, mark the notches, centered 10" from each end of the keel slat. At the same time, mark the notches for

A 6"-wide blank is ideal for laying out the slats so you can nest the parts.

Jatoba is very brittle and prone to splintering, so attention to grain direction while routing is essential to avoid tearout.

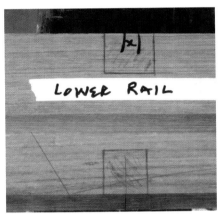

Carefully mark the notches for the rails. Here, a lower rail blank is lying on top of the stretcher blank.

Strive for a snug fit between the stretcher and lower rail.

Jatoba Bench

NO.	ITEM	DIMENSIONS (INCHES)			MATERIAL
		T	W	L	
8	Regular slats	1	$2\frac{1}{4}$	48	Jatoba
1	Keel slat	1	$3\frac{1}{4}$	48	Jatoba
4	Legs	$1\frac{1}{2}$	$2\frac{1}{4}$	17	Jatoba
1	Stretcher	$1\frac{1}{2}$	$3\frac{1}{2}$	35	Jatoba
2	Top rails	$1\frac{1}{8}$	$2\frac{1}{4}$	14	Jatoba
2	Bottom rails	$1\frac{1}{4}$	$2\frac{3}{4}$	14	Jatoba
16	Spacers	$\frac{1}{2}$	1	1	Ebony
4	Plugs	$\frac{5}{8}$ dia.		$\frac{1}{4}$	Ebony
4	Plugs	$\frac{5}{8}$ dia.		$\frac{1}{4}$	Jatoba
Hardware					
2	Threaded rods	$\frac{1}{4}$-20		12	Stainless steel
4	Nuts	$\frac{1}{4}$			Stainless steel
4	Washers	$\frac{1}{4}$			Stainless steel
2	Lag screws			2	Stainless steel
2	Lag screws			$2\frac{1}{2}$	Stainless steel

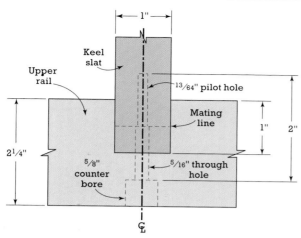

BRIDLE JOINT MATING UPPER RAIL AND KEEL SLAT

Keel slat

Upper rail

1"

¹³⁄₆₄" pilot hole

Mating line

1"

2"

2¹⁄₄"

⅝" counter bore

⁵⁄₁₆" through hole

C̵L

the lower stretcher, as the keel slat and stretcher must be aligned. Also mark the top and bottom rails for their notches. Raise your table saw blade to ¹⁄₂", make a test cut and adjust as necessary. Machine the notches in the keel slat and top rails. Sneak up on the final width, checking as you go for a snug fit. Reset the table saw blade height to 1³⁄₈" and machine the two notch cuts in the stretcher, along with the notches in the bottom rails. Test-fit and clean up the notches with a shoulder plane or chisel.

With the notches completed, machine the curved edges of the keel slat and stretcher, repeating the process used for the slats – i.e. band saw, template-rout, cut to length and sand smooth.

Make a simple jig with a 30° notch as shown on the next page (top left). Use the slat template and jig to set up your drill

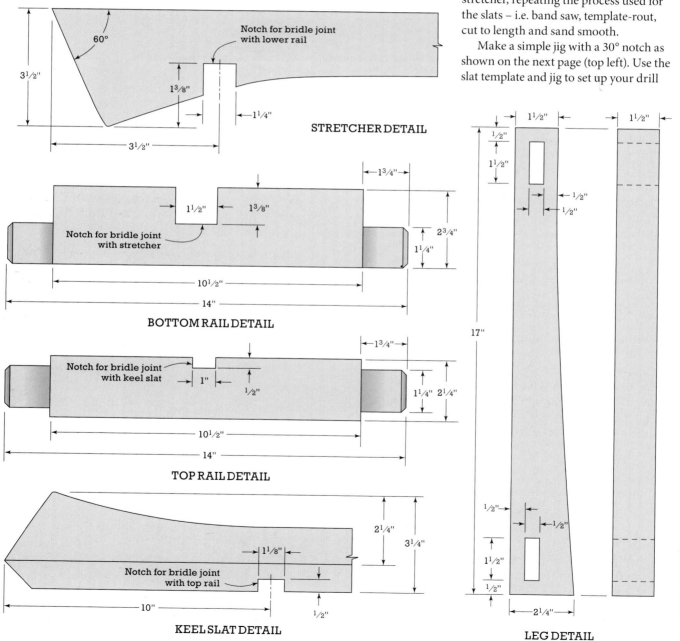

60°

3¹⁄₂"

Notch for bridle joint with lower rail

1³⁄₈"

1¹⁄₄"

3¹⁄₂"

STRETCHER DETAIL

1³⁄₄"

1¹⁄₂"   1³⁄₈"

Notch for bridle joint with stretcher

2³⁄₄"

1¹⁄₄"

10¹⁄₂"

14"

BOTTOM RAIL DETAIL

1³⁄₄"

Notch for bridle joint with keel slat

1"

¹⁄₂"

1¹⁄₄"   2¹⁄₄"

10¹⁄₂"

14"

TOP RAIL DETAIL

2¹⁄₄"

3¹⁄₄"

1¹⁄₈"

Notch for bridle joint with top rail

10"

¹⁄₂"

KEEL SLAT DETAIL

1¹⁄₂"   1¹⁄₂"

¹⁄₂"

1¹⁄₂"

¹⁄₂"

¹⁄₂"

17"

¹⁄₂"   ¹⁄₂"

1¹⁄₂"

¹⁄₂"

2¹⁄₄"

LEG DETAIL

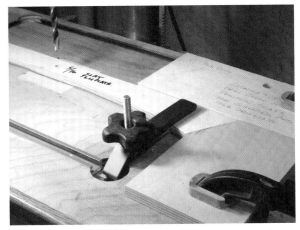

Set up to drill 5/16" holes in the slats. Both ends of the slats are secured with hold-downs for this critical operation.

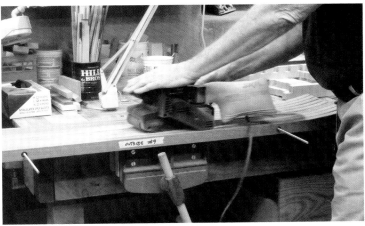

I use my ancient (and very loud) belt sander to level the slats. This operation requires a light touch and good hearing protection.

press. Drill 5/16" holes in the slats. Note that the two outside slats also receive 1/2"-deep counterbored holes, centered on the previously cut 5/16" holes. Use a 5/8" Forstner bit for these counterbored holes, and drill them while the slats are still in the clamps.

When all the slats are drilled, gang the slats together, secured with two 1/4"-20 threaded rods (about 15" long) and corresponding 1/4" washers and nuts. Number the slats for later re-assembly and sand them as a unit, first with a belt sander and finally with your random-orbit sander (ROS). Next, ease the edges with a 3/16" roundover bit at the router table. As before, pay attention to grain direction. Finally, sand all slats individually with your ROS, working up to #220 grit. (I find that Mirka's Abranet does a quick job on this tough wood.) There should be no sharp edges, except for the notches in the keel slat. I finished the process by hand-sanding with #600 grit.

Machine a piece of ebony to 1" × 1" × 12" and slice 16½"-spacers at the band saw. Each spacer receives a 5/16" hole, centered by using a jig. This is a critical operation as the spacers must align perfectly during assembly. While at the band saw, cut four 3/8"-long ebony plugs using a 5/8" plug cutter. Also cut four jatoba plugs, which will be used later.

The top is now ready for assembly. Add washers and nuts to one end of the two threaded rods, with the nuts threaded just enough to be flush with the rod ends. Insert the rods through one of the outside slats so that the washer/nut

After machining a piece of ebony to 1" × 1" × 12", slice 16½"-spacers at the band saw. And make a few extra, just in case.

Drill 5/16" holes in the center of the spacers. I made a simple bird's mouth, along with a 90° jig, to secure the spacers during this operation.

To start assembly, insert a rod through one of the outside slats so the washer and nuts are recessed in your counterbored holes. Slide on a spacer. Repeat.

Lay out the mortises on only one leg, which you'll use to set up the stops on your mortiser – no need to mark the others.

I used the horizontal mortiser with a $^1/_2$" spiral-upcut bit on my Robland X-31 to machine the mortises in the legs

Here, you can see where the plunge bit will enter the cut.

Use a chisel to square your mortise corners as necessary.

The fit of the milled tenons is critical to success, so check them with a dial caliper.

combinations are recessed in the counterbored holes. Slide a spacer onto each rod, add a slat and repeat until all the slats are in place.

Add the washers and nuts to the other end of the threaded rods and snug the short end using a $^7/_{16}$" nut driver. (I discovered that not all $^7/_{16}$"-nut drivers will fit in the $^5/_8$" holes. I had success with a $^1/_4$"-drive set.) Measure the width of the top. You may find it somewhat different than the 13" dimension because slight differences in thickness of the slats or spacers are cumulative. In any case, the final width is important for cutting the threaded rod. Subtract $^1/_2$" from the measured top width and record this number.

Disassemble the top and use a hacksaw to cut the threaded rods to that length. File the ends of the rods to eliminate any sharp or jagged edges, and test

them with the nuts to ensure they thread easily. Assemble the top as before and tighten the nuts "finger tight." Check and adjust the spacers so they are all aligned, then tighten the nuts firmly. Using a waterproof glue or epoxy, glue in the ebony plugs you made earlier. When cured, cut off the excess, being careful not to mar the slats. Sand smooth to complete the top assembly.

Making the Legs

You previously machined leg blanks to $1^1/_2$" × $2^1/_4$". As shown on the drawing (page 38), the legs taper from $1^1/_2$" at the top to $2^1/_4$" at the bottom. Make a template of the fair curve, just as you did with the slats. Attach the template to the leg blanks with double-stick tape before machining them on the band saw. Because they are $1^1/_2$" thick, instead of

using a pattern bit on the router I used my oscillating spindle sander to bring them to final dimension. Ease the edges with a $^3/_{16}$" roundover bit. As with the slats, consider the grain orientation in this operation.

Mark the locations of the leg mortises and cut the mortises. I set up the horizontal slot mortiser on my Robland X-31 with a $^1/_2$" spiral upcut bit. I milled all eight mortises and squared the corners with a sharp bench chisel.

Now for the rails. Note that the top and bottom rails are quite different. First, they have different thicknesses. I designed the bottom rails somewhat larger because the legs taper, and because the stretcher is robust. Also, note from the drawing that the tenons are located differently. The top rail must align with the top of the legs in order to form a flat surface and support the top. Thus the shoulder cut for the top rail tenon is ½" to match the topmost mortise cut. To give the mortises symmetry, the bottom mortise is placed ½" from the bottom of the leg. However, the rail should not extend to the floor. To solve this, I offset the tenon on the bottom rail, omitting a shoulder cut in the process. Thus the lower rail begins ½" above the floor.

Machine ½"-thick tenons on both rails. I mounted a slot-cutting blade on the shaper and adjusted it to make the tenon cheek cuts. Make the shoulder cuts on the band saw and make final adjustments with a shoulder plane or bench chisel. "Dress" the ends of the through-tenons with hand-cut chamfers. Next, drill ⅝"-counterbored holes ½" deep into the bottom of each rail, centered below the bridle-joint notches. Drill pilot holes for ¼" stainless steel lag screws to secure the top and stretcher. As with the slats, sand all pieces through #220 grit with your ROS, then finish by hand-sanding with #600 grit.

With all pieces machined, it is time for a trial assembly. Put together the leg assemblies and add the stretcher. Set the top in place. Check that all bridle joints are fully in place. Perform any last-

I finished the end of each through-tenon by clamping the workpiece into my bench vise, then clamped on a jig to hand-cut the chamfers.

minute tweaking as necessary. Glue and clamp the mortise-and-tenon joints on the legs and rails.

Finish & Final Assembly

Apply several coats of boiled linseed oil on all pieces, along with a top coat of wax. Complete the assembly by adding the lag screws to secure the bridle joints, then glue the jatoba plugs in the counterbored holes. Sand flush and finish with boiled linseed oil and wax. If you are planning to ship the bench to a client, omit the jatoba plugs and send the pieces flat. Add instructions and lag screws for the client to perform the final assembly.

The leg assembly should be test fit to make sure all the bridle joints are correct. Tweak as necessary before glue-up.

Apply several coats of boiled linseed oil, and a topcoat of wax. Oil increases the contrast between jatoba and ebony. The spacers and plugs, seen in the inset photos, add visual interest.

Esherick-Style Stool

BY CHUCK BENDER

Looking at Wharton Esherick's furniture, it's easy to see how he brought nature into his designs. I'm not talking about how he simply carved abstract turkey buzzards on the front of an Arts & Crafts-style desk, but how, once he began to view furniture as sculpture, the pieces themselves abstractly represented natural elements.

Like many studio woodworkers, Esherick developed one product that kept the cash flowing. In Esherick's case that was his famous three-legged stool. He made them from scraps of figured material laying about the shop, making each random in shape and size. Esherick sculpted the seats while shop apprentices turned the legs and did the joinery.

The design of the stools is simple – slender legs with a light, draping seat floating atop. When I look at the stools, I am reminded of reeds or rushes by a pond in autumn; the willowy reeds stretch upward supporting a fallen leaf. This is the imagery I hope I've captured in my interpretation.

Time to Design

For a period furniture maker, the hardest part of tackling a project that's inspired by an existing piece is resisting the urge to simply copy it. That goes double for a project that isn't of a period design.

I began with a general concept in mind: a low-back, three-legged stool that would work as seating at my kitchen counter. As the opening photo shows, the concept changed slightly. The final version came about after much deliberation, contemplation and plain old fear.

Esherick had it easy. His stools had three legs, and the seats were generally small. They played perfectly into his love of asymmetry.

Whenever you add a back to any type of seating furniture, the first thing you need to do is increase the size of the seat. If you don't, the surface area will be too small when used for its intended purpose. Also, there might be too little material to support the back if the seat is too small.

For my larger seat, I bypassed the scrap bin and grabbed a board that was about 10½" wide and some plywood for a pattern. I then started sketching out an asymmetrical seat. My seat demanded a fourth leg; the legs and stretchers mimic those on Esherick's stools. My intent was to design and build something he might have actually made.

Time to Choose

With a basic pattern in hand, it's time to look at the figure in the board and decide from which part to cut the seat.

Consider a few things when selecting your material. Figure is of paramount concern when making something this simple in design. Make sure it gives the piece a sense of visual balance, while not being overwhelming.

Once you've decided on the figure, look at the board's grain structure. The more figured the board, the less stable and strong the seat. At one end I had an off-center crotch. In the middle, the grain was fairly straight, with some curl. At the other end, the board had a knot and some good curl: I chose the knotty end.

The crotch end of the board would have made a more spectacular seat, but because it was off-center, one of the holes for a leg would have passed right through a section where the grain direction was almost vertical, making it too weak for a leg joint.

The middle of the board was just too plain for my taste. By staying off the knot, I got a seat with interesting figure that is structurally sound.

After laying out and cutting the seat, I turned back to the pattern to figure out leg-hole placement. The holes need to be in far enough from the edge of the seat so as not to weaken the board, but not so far that they end up too close together. I made the holes in the seat asymmetrical in keeping with Esherick's style.

Once you have the leg holes marked, drive a small finish nail through the plywood pattern at the center of each location. Align the pattern on the bottom of the seat blank and tap the nails to mark the center of the legs.

Time to Drill

By drilling the holes before shaping the seat or turning the legs, you'll find the ¾" holes easier to drill, and you can test-fit the tops of the legs as you turn them.

The angles on Esherick's stool legs varied quite a bit. Some were more vertical while others splayed outward to give the stool a greater sense of drama. In choosing the angles for my stool, I used a few offcut sticks, cut to the approximate height of the stool. With the seat inverted on my bench, I held the sticks at an angle that suited my eye.

Choosing your figure and grain direction is crucial for a sturdy stool. The nails in the pattern help locate the center of the leg holes.

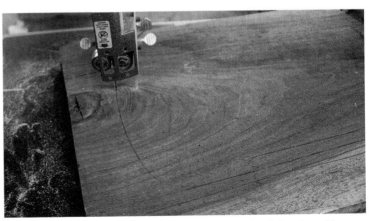

Careful placement of the pattern allows the seat to be defect-free. The band saw makes short work of roughing out the seat blank.

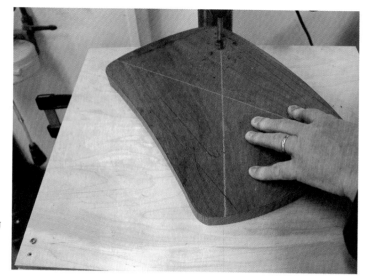

Using a shop-made jig, the leg holes are easily bored at the selected angle.

In order to drill the holes in the seat blank, there has to be a way of referencing the blank to get the legs splaying at relatively the same angle. Esherick may have eschewed symmetry, but having the legs on the stool splay at four different angles would have been a bit much, even for him.

I made a simple jig for the drill press from two pieces of plywood and a scrap of 2×4. By placing the scrap between the plywood along one edge, you create an auxiliary table that tilts toward the front of the drill press. If you like more or less splay on your stool's legs, modify the size of the spacer.

Mark a centerline that divides the slope into left and right halves. This is the line you use to set the orientation of the seat to keep the angles consistent on all four legs. Align the centerline with the drill bit on the press then clamp the jig in place.

Draw diagonal lines across the bottom of the seat through the centers of the leg holes. Now you merely have to line up the center marks with the drill bit and the diagonal line with the centerline on the jig and drill away.

Time to Turn

Esherick made many legs from hickory, oak and ash, but I didn't limit myself to his choices. I've always liked the strong contrast of maple – particularly when it's curly – and walnut (which happened to have been Esherick's favorite wood). If you have other woods that you favor, use them. Just remember: When choosing a species for your legs, make sure that it can stand up to flexing under the weight of an occupant and to the abrasion of actually being dragged across a floor.

Turning the legs is a fairly simple process. Begin with a quick layout stick to ensure all your legs come out the same

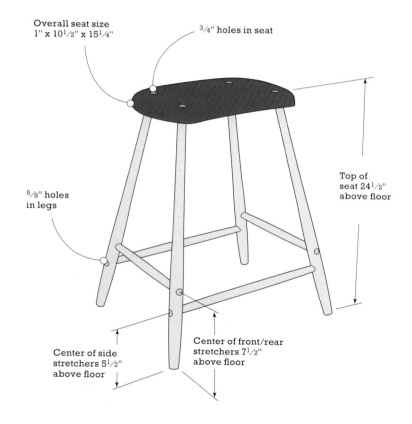

Overall seat size
1" x 10½" x 15¼"

¾" holes in seat

Top of
seat 24½"
above floor

⅝" holes
in legs

Center of side
stretchers 5½"
above floor

Center of front/rear
stretchers 7½"
above floor

Esherick-Style Stool

NO.	ITEM	DIMENSIONS (INCHES)			MATERIAL
		T	W	L	
1	Seat	1	10½	15¼	Walnut
4	Legs	1¼	1¼	26	Maple
1	Front stretcher	1¼	1¼	18⅝*	Maple
1	Back stretcher	1¼	1¼	18*	Maple
2	Side stretchers	1¼	1¼	13¼*	Maple
*Add 2" to length for turning					

After turning the leg blank to a $1\frac{1}{4}$"-diameter cylinder, use the layout stick to plot the top and bottom, and the middle of the swelled part of the leg.

A fairly simple turning trick to get consistent sizes is to use a wrench as a caliper.

Work from the largest diameter toward the smaller diameters when turning. This is particularly important when turning the slender tenons on the stretchers.

size. The stick doesn't have to be much more than a scrap cut a little longer than the final leg length, with hash marks showing the top, bottom and middle of the swelled area (on mine, that's $6\frac{1}{2}$" from the bottom).

The only other sizes you need to determine are the final diameters at each of the three points on your stick. On my stool the top of the leg is $\frac{3}{4}$", the bottom is $\frac{7}{8}$" and the middle of the swell is $1\frac{1}{4}$" in diameter.

Once the blanks are sawn to size, mark the centers on the ends and chuck them in the lathe. I usually make my blanks about $\frac{1}{16}$" oversized in thickness and width to give me a little wiggle room in case my stock warps or I don't get things perfectly centered.

Start by turning the entire blank to a $1\frac{1}{4}$"-diameter cylinder. Hold the layout stick to the cylinder and transfer the hash marks. Using open-end wrenches of the appropriate size as calipers, turn the ends down to the proper diameters. All that's left is to flow from the middle of the swell out to the ends.

To get all four legs approximately the same size, I turned the first to size and shape then used it as a reference as I turned the remaining legs. I still transfer all the marks from the layout stick, but the comparison ensures I'm not making the subsequent legs larger or smaller in diameter. Just like using the layout stick to mark all the important points on the leg, using the first turned leg gives you a single benchmark from which to work.

Time to Stretch

With the legs turned, it's time to dry-fit them in the seat, and to figure out the angles and placement of the stretcher holes. I've spaced the stretchers 1" above and below the swell centerline.

To figure out the angles use more scraps. Because the front stretcher acts as a footrest, I positioned it (and the back stretcher) below the centerline.

Clamp the scraps to the legs referencing off the stretcher lines. Use a sliding bevel to approximate the angle, and check that the left and right sides are the same. Transfer the angles to a layout stick and label them so you don't get confused later.

Sliding bevel

Clamp scraps to the dry-assembled base and set a bevel to the centerline of the leg. This will be the angle at which you will drill the holes for the stretchers.

The Design Process

Designing a Wharton Esherick-style stool started long before I milled any lumber or made a sketch. It began with a concept. But how one turns a concept into reality is something of a mystery to many. Most folks begin with a plan, perhaps from a book or magazine, that may or may not have a cutlist. The key thing is that it's something tangible. Many never take the leap of making something that only exists in their head.

While Esherick stools don't exist only in my head, I didn't have access to one of his stools or to measured drawings; I had photos and a concept. For me, the design process usually starts with a layout stick but this project doesn't work well with section drawings. Without knowing the leg angles, SketchUp wasn't the optimal choice, either. While I tried a couple of rough perspective sketches, a mock-up seemed in order.

My first concept kept Esherick's three legs. But because my original thought included a back on the stool, I started sketching out a larger, squarish seat rather than his more triangular, rounded look so there would be room to sit on the stool once it was done. I also wanted to be sure to capture Esherick's sense of lightness.

My first seat had arched sides and arched around the back to accommodate a curved crest rail; it resembled a stylized Windsor D-shaped seat. Using 8/4 poplar, I hacked out a seat, turned three legs and drilled holes. With the first mock-up dry-assembled, it was easy to see that something wasn't right. The top was heavy, the legs looked spindly and I still had to figure out a back. A new design was in order.

I first had to lighten the look of the seat. I narrowed the depth of the pattern but kept it rectangular to give me enough width to include a back. As the seat narrowed, it was evident that the stool needed a fourth leg. It wouldn't otherwise be stable. I grabbed more poplar, hacked out another seat, turned an additional leg, drilled more holes and roughed out a seat. The new mock-up had the lightness and balance I was looking for, but left me wondering about the addition of a back.

At this point, it was best to jump into the real project. This allowed me to refine the majority of the stool and gave me more time to think about the back design. As the project took shape, the reality of adding a back continued to disappear. The more I worked on it and the more I looked at the light appearance, it became clear that adding a low back would do little to improve the design; it would make the seat appear clunky.

If you have a project idea, you might just have to jump in and give things a try. Sometimes your standard method of work just won't cut it when you're trying to work out a design.

You don't have to work out the problems on your good lumber. Don't be afraid to grab cheap scrap material and start hacking away.

Rough assemble the stool and trim the tenons close so the wedge placement can be marked.

You don't need to be exact nor do you need to work to final finish to get an idea of what works and what doesn't about a design. And you don't need to get stuck in one track or the other. If part of the project can be dealt with using a layout stick or SketchUp drawing, and another part using a foam or a wooden mock-up, you need to dive in and give it a try. Your design, as well as your woodworking skills, will benefit from the experience.

Making a jig to drill the stretcher holes can be easily done with a small piece of 2×4. Drill a $1^{1}/_{4}$" hole from both sides then rip the piece to $^{11}/_{16}$" thick to create a trough in which to place the leg for drilling.

The side-stretcher angles are measured the same way. Because my seat is rectangular, the stretcher angles on the sides are different than on the front and back. Pay attention when drilling the holes because the legs are handed.

With the scrap boards clamped in place, take the rough measurements for the stretcher lengths. On my stool the side stretchers are of equal length while the front stretcher is longer than the back.

Once you have the lengths calculated, turn the stretchers. I made mine overlong and made sure the ends were $^{5}/_{8}$" in diameter over the last $2^{1}/_{2}$".

To drill the holes at the proper angle on the drill press, you need a way to hold them consistently. I made a simple jig from a 2×4 offcut. On both ends measure and draw a center mark 1" off the back face and centered on the width. Set up a $1^{1}/_{4}$" Forstner bit in the drill press. Clamp the piece into a handscrew and drill from both ends until the holes meet in the middle. The handscrew ensures the piece is held perpendicular to the table and provides a safe way to drill the deep holes.

With the hole bored all the way through the 2×4, rip the piece to $1^{1}/_{16}$" thick, referencing off the back face. This

Tilt the drill press table to the proper angle using an angle layout stick.

With the drill bit centered on the jig, drill the front and back stretcher holes.

After tilting the drill press table to the second angle, insert a stretcher into the hole in the leg, place the assembly in the jig and drill the side-stretcher holes through the legs. You'll need to drill two legs with the table tilted left and two with it tilted right.

makes a jig that cradles the legs and allows a stretcher to be inserted in order to drill the second hole perpendicular to the first, and it helps minimize tearout as the drill bit exits the leg.

Chuck a ⅝" drill bit into the press and use the layout stick to set the angles. Center the jig under the bit and drill the first holes through the legs. Insert a stretcher into the holes and readjust the table to the proper angle. Make sure the jig is still centered. Now drill the second hole in each leg. Complete the holes on all legs.

Time to Grind

It's time to shape the seat. This can be done with hand tools, power tools or a combination. I chose to use a combination.

I began by sketching a rectangular shape that encompasses all four leg holes. This represents the transition point from concave to convex shape.

The seat is dished out about ¼" deep. If you plan on making multiples of the same stool – not very Esherick-like, but I can understand the need – you may want to use a Forstner bit to drill some depth guides so you are consistent; otherwise, dive in.

I set up a mini-grinder to hog out the bulk of the waste on the seat. You could also use a scorp and round spokeshave to accomplish the same.

After roughing out the dished area of the seat, I moved to rounding off the outer edge. The idea is to give the seat a drooping appearance.

To lighten the look of the seat, the underside is chamfered. To achieve the natural drooping-leaf appearance, the chamfers arch toward the top, following the shape created when rounding off the outside edge of the seat. The more you chamfer under the seat, the thinner the look; just don't go too far or you'll start to reduce the material surrounding the legs. For this work, I use spokeshaves.

Once the seat is roughed in on both top and bottom, I switch to a sander to smooth out all the bumps. I then round all the edges with a spokeshave, but you can also do this with a sander or grinder. Don't bother to take the seat to final smoothness. There will be cleanup to do after the stool is assembled.

Time to Glue

Dry-fit the entire stool one last time. This allows you to cut off legs or stretchers that are just far too long. You want them to protrude through the joints but not so far that you can use them for hanging plants.

At this point, mark how the wedges will be inserted into the joints. I also take the time to mark each part so they go back in the same places during final assembly.

Disassemble the stool and cut kerfs into all the legs and stretchers for wedges. Often, I'll do this with a dovetail saw if there aren't too many, or at the band saw if I have more. Just don't cut the kerfs too deep or you'll see them on the insides of the joints after assembly.

Esherick typically used wedge mate-

Attach the seat topside up to a stick with a couple of screws through it. This allows you to secure the work in a vise for grinding and shaping with hand tools.

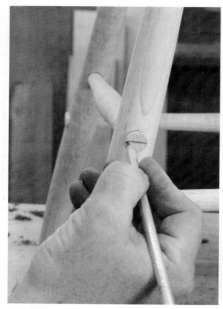

Taking time to mark the placement and orientation of each wedge will save frustration later.

At the band saw, cut wedges from a scrap.

Using the stretchers and legs as a pattern, it's easy to trim the wedges to final width.

rial of the same color, but I wanted more contrast; I used walnut. At the band saw, make a series of wedge-shape cuts into a scrap, then cut them off in groups. Don't worry at this point if the wedges are too wide for the joints; they can be trimmed just before insertion.

Use a leg and stretcher to mark off the width of the wedges. Using an offcut as a cutting board, trim each wedge to width with a sharp chisel. A touch of glue on the tip of each wedge ensures it stays in place once driven home.

Using a small acid brush, glue each joint and begin by assembling the base. Next, glue the leg-to-seat joints. Tap the seat into place, checking to make sure it remains parallel to the floor. This is easily done by measuring to the flat part of the seat's underside and adjusting until you get the same measurement.

Install the wedges, then use a file, chisel or sander to trim the joints flush and flow them into the legs and seat.

Time to Back Out

When my stool was fully assembled, I looked at the overall appearance. It had achieved all the goals I set forth at the beginning of the project: It was light in appearance and harkened back to Esherick's own stools.

The concern at this point was how

a back would change the balance. The seat was larger than many of Esherick's stools, but still on the small size for a seating piece with a back.

After mocking up a few different versions, some taller and others shorter, I decided a back was only going to make the stool look clunky and heavy. So I dropped it.

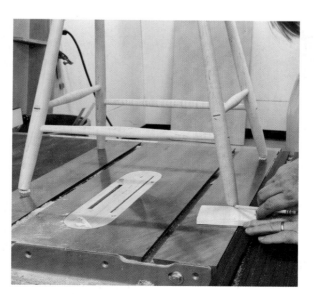

All that remained was leveling and finish prep. I placed the stool on the table saw and made shims to temporarily level it. Using a ½" scrap of plywood, I scribed around all four legs and trimmed them off with a handsaw at the bench. If your stool still doesn't sit perfectly level, a little fiddling with a chisel or rasp makes short work of that.

Time to Finish

Finishing in the Esherick style isn't very difficult at all; he used tung oil.

After sanding the entire stool to #180 grit, I rubbed on a few coats of tung oil and allowed it to fully cure between coats. I also lightly sanded between coats with #320-grit sandpaper and wiped the entire stool down with a tack cloth prior to subsequent coats. At the end, I used #0000 steel wool to rub out the finish then applied a light coat of paste wax. The wax isn't necessary on an oil finish, but it leaves the surfaces smooth and tactile.

Not only were Esherick's stools and other pieces very touchable, they were fluid. It's that fluidity that I sought in my stool. I even found it in the design process. Stepping outside my regular sphere of work helped me remember not to get locked into one train of thought or one method of work. Sometimes it's liberating to go where the work and the wood take you.

Shim the stool on a level surface and use a scrap of plywood to scribe all four legs. Saw to the lines and it might just be perfect the first time.

Moravian Stool

BY CHRISTOPHER SCHWARZ

One highlight of a visit to historic Old Salem in North Carolina is the beautiful Moravian furniture and woodwork in the village's buildings. My favorite piece in the town is a small, sturdy stool that shows up in many of the buildings. The costumed interpreters sit, kneel, stand or even saw on reproductions of this stool every day.

This form is also common in rural Europe, especially in eastern Bavaria, which is close to the origin of the Moravians in the Czech Republic. In Europe, it's also common to see this stool with a back – sometimes carved – which turns it into a chair.

But the best part of the stool is that it requires about $10 in wood and two days in the shop to build – and it has a lot of fun operations: tapered octagons, sliding dovetails, compound leg splays and wedged through-tenons. And by building this stool, you'll be about halfway home to being able to build a Windsor or Welsh chair.

This particular stool is based on originals owned by Old Salem that are made from poplar. The stools are remarkably lightweight – less than 4 lbs. Like many original stools, the top of many Old Salem stools have split because of their cross-grain construction. Despite the split, the stools remain rock-solid thanks to sliding dovetail battens under the seat. I like to think of the split as just another kind of necessary wood movement.

Here's how the stool goes together: The thin top is pierced by two sliding-dovetail sockets. Two battens fit into those sockets. The legs pierce both the battens and the stool's top, and they are wedged in place through the top. This is the cross-grain joint that will make the top split in time.

The best place to begin construction is with the legs.

Geometry 101

The legs are tapered octagons. They are 1⅝" square at the top and 1" square at the foot. The top of the leg has an 1⅜"-diameter × 1½"-long round tenon. To make the legs, first mark the 1⅝" octagon on the top of the leg and the 1" octagon at the foot. See "Octagons Made Easy" on the next page.

With your octagons drawn, saw each leg into a tapered square – 1⅝" at the top and 1" at the foot. I cut these tapers on the band saw, though I've also done it with a jack plane.

With the legs tapered, you can connect the corners of your two octagons with a pencil and a straightedge. Then it's just a matter of planing the four corners down to your pencil lines, which creates an octagon.

Now turn the tenons on the top of each leg. The tenons are 1⅜" in diameter and 1½" long. This is a quick operation

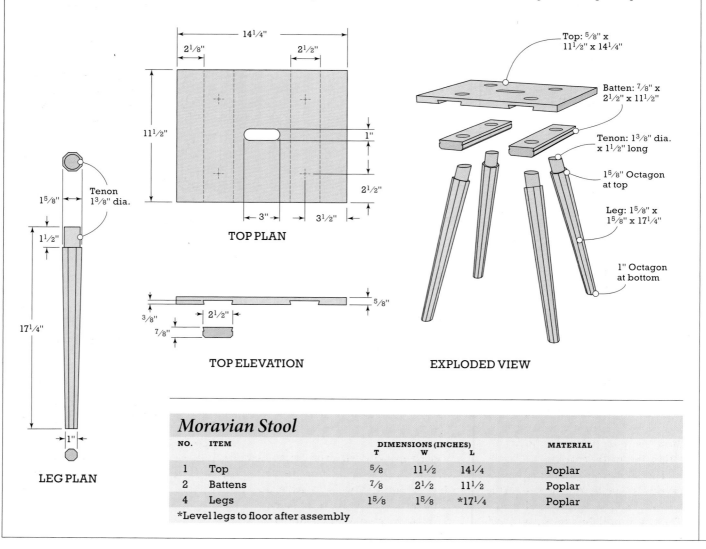

LEG PLAN

TOP PLAN

TOP ELEVATION

EXPLODED VIEW

No.	Item	Dimensions (inches)			Material
		T	W	L	
1	Top	⅝	11½	14¼	Poplar
2	Battens	⅞	2½	11½	Poplar
4	Legs	1⅝	1⅝	*17¼	Poplar

Moravian Stool

*Level legs to floor after assembly

with a parting tool. Measure your tenons with dial calipers to ensure they are exactly 1$\frac{3}{8}$" or just slightly less. If they are even slightly fat, they won't go in.

Big Sliding Dovetails

Many beginners are intimated by sliding dovetails because they are hard to fit, especially when made by machine. It seems to take a lot of hammering to get the joint seated without gaps.

When you make them by hand, you can build in a little forgiveness that makes them both easy to assemble and tight. The trick? A shoulder plane. But I'm getting ahead of myself. First we have to cut the long and wide socket on the underside of the stool's top.

Fetch your sliding bevel and set it to 16° off of 90° (or 106°). Lock it. Tight. That is the only angle you need for the entire project – even the compound splay of the legs.

The 16° is the angle of the walls of the sliding dovetail. Lay out the locations of the battens so they are 2$\frac{1}{8}$" from the ends of the top. The dovetail socket is $\frac{3}{8}$" deep, 2$\frac{1}{2}$" wide at the bottom and has 16° splayed walls. Lay out the sockets on the underside and edges of the top.

Now you need to saw the angled walls of the sockets. With short sliding dovetails (for drawer blades, for example) I'll just kerf them freehand. But because these sockets are 11$\frac{1}{2}$" long, I make a guide for my handsaw.

The guide is just a piece of 2"-square scrap that has one edge sawn or planed to 16°. I clamp the scrap to the underside of the bottom and saw the walls by pressing the sawplate against the guide while stroking forward and back.

Remove the majority of the waste with a chisel and mallet. Then finish the bottom of the sockets to their final depth of $\frac{3}{8}$" using a router plane.

Shape the Battens to Fit

The battens have the complementary shape cut into them. Unlike the sockets, there is very little material to remove to make the male section of the joint – just little slivers on the edges.

The dovetail is $\frac{3}{8}$" thick and has 16° bevels. Lay out the $\frac{3}{8}$" thickness on the two edges and two ends of the batten. Then use your sliding bevel to scribe the

To make an octagon, set your compass for the distance between the center point of your square and one corner.

For the small octagon at the foot, mark the square you want to turn into an octagon, reset your compass and repeat the process.

Octagons Made Easy

Making a proper octagon is a mystery for many beginning woodworkers, but it is easy. All you need is a compass, a center point and four corners of a square.
1. Set the compass to the distance between one corner and the center point of the square you wish to make into an octagon.
2. Place the point of the compass at one corner and strike an arc across the square.
3. Repeat this process at the other three corners of your square.
4. The resulting pattern looks a bit like a flower. The eight points where the arcs intersect the square are the points of your octagon. Plane down to those lines and you have a well-proportioned octagon.

Here you can see the arcs of the octagon and how they create the facets of your octagon.

16° angle. The angle should touch the corner of the batten and your $\frac{3}{8}$" scribe line. Then you just have to remove the material in the two right triangles created by your pencil.

There are lots of ways to do this, but the most straightforward is to remove the majority of the waste with a shoulder plane (or a rabbet plane) and tease the waste out of the corner with a fine handsaw or chisel.

Plane down to your layout lines and clean up the joint for a test-fit. Decide which way the joint will go together and compare the ends of the batten to the sockets in your top. When both ends of a

Tenon the legs. Turn a 1$\frac{1}{2}$" long by 1$\frac{3}{8}$"-diameter tenon on the top of each leg after you've finished planing the octagons.

The 16° guide is made from scrap and is clamped to the underside of the stool's top. An 8-point crosscut handsaw was used to make these four kerfs.

A chisel can remove waste much faster than a router plane. Just keep an eye on the grain so it doesn't split below the final depth of the socket.

Router planes excel at making housed joints perfectly flat. You could do this work with a chisel, but it would be a fussy process.

Legging Up

By far the most stressful part of the project is "legging up" – where you bore the compound-angle holes through the battens and seat. Luckily, there are some chairmaking tricks that make this process a snap.

batten will fit in their socket, the temptation is to hammer it home. Resist.

Instead, return to your bench vise and clamp your batten in place. Mark the sliding dovetail about 1½" from both ends of the batten. Then make stopped shavings between those two pencil marks until the plane stops cutting. Repeat this process on the other 16° walls.

These stopped shavings hollow out the middle of the sliding dovetail, which makes fitting the joint much easier.

Now use a mallet to drive the battens

in place. No glue. You should be able to get the batten to slide in place with the same sort of force you would use for chopping dovetail waste. If you are whaling on the batten and denting it, your joint is too tight. Remove the batten and plane a little more off.

Once the battens are fit, plane a ³⁄₁₆" × ³⁄₁₆" chamfer on their long edges to reduce the physical and visual weight of the stool.

The first trick is to ignore the fact that the legs are inserted at a compound angle – called rake and splay. Instead, lay out the leg angle from the center of an "X" drawn between the locations of the four leg mortises. By working out from the center point of the seat, you can drill the holes at a single angle. The resulting hole produces a compound angle, but by working from the center point, you only have to worry about one angle, which is what we call the "resultant angle" in chairmaking.

And here's the best part: For this stool, the resultant angle is 16° – the same angle setting as the sliding dovetail.

First step: Lay out the center point of the four leg mortises on the underside of the assembled seat. The center point of

Here's the little triangular section that creates the dovetail, which was cut with a shoulder plane. The waste in the corner can be removed using a saw or chisel.

There is so much friction in assembling a sliding dovetail that it's best to hollow out the middle of the joint with a few "stopped shavings" along the joint's bevel.

each leg hole is 2½" from the long edges and 3½" from the ends. Draw a big "X" on the underside that connects these four points – yes, it's a pain to draw because of the battens.

Now you have a choice: Chuck up a 1⅜" Forstner in your brace or cordless drill and eyeball the angle using a sliding bevel placed on the "X." This is how I usually do it with chairs.

Or take the chicken road and do it on the drill press. Here, I demonstrate the chicken method. Make a small platform that bevels the seat at 16° on your drill press's table. Clamp the platform to the drill press. Chuck a 1⅜" Forstner in your drill press. Line up the long line of your "X" with the shank of your bit and the post of your drill press. That will ensure the hole is at the true "resultant angle." Drill through the seat and take it slow so you don't splinter the seat when the bit breaks through.

Rotate the seat and repeat the process for the three other holes.

Brief Detours Before Assembly

These stools have a handle in the middle that makes them easy to carry around. This handhold is 1" × 3" and runs parallel to the grain. Bore it out using a brace and bit or a drill press and finish the shape with rasps.

Another thing you need to do before assembly is to make some 1⅜"-wide wedges to drive into the tenons on the legs. I use wedges that have a 6° included angle and are about 1¼" long. Make them from hardwood – I usually use oak – and make them by splitting or sawing. (I've provided a short video on popular-woodworking.com/dec12 that shows how I do this on a band saw.)

If your tenons fit tightly in the mortises, you will need to saw kerfs in the tenons so the wedges will go in. If your tenons are loose, you can split the tenon with a chisel after driving the legs home.

Last detail: Chamfer the rim of your tenons with a rasp. This will help prevent your seat from splintering when you whack the legs in place.

The platform raises the seat to the 16° resultant angle. The pencil lines ensure that the angle is in relation to the center-point of the seat.

Wedging the tenons will keep them tight even after the glue fails. To prevent splitting, the kerf in the tenon is perpendicular to the grain of the seat.

Traditional Glue

I use hide glue for most things, but especially chairs and stools. Any household article that will take abuse and might require repair is an excellent candidate for hide glue because it is reversible and easily repaired.

Brush the glue on the mortise and the tenon and drive the legs home. If you sawed a kerf in the tenon, align the kerf so it is perpendicular to the grain of the stool's top. If you don't do this, the wedge will split the seat.

Drive the wedges home. Stop tapping them when they stop moving deeper into the tenon. Wait for the glue to dry, then saw the tenons flush to the seat.

Cut the feet so they sit flat on the floor – popularwoodworking.com/dec has a link to a story that explains how to do this. Then break all the sharp edges on the stool with sandpaper.

Many of these stools were painted. I applied three coats of General Finishes' Tuscan Red milk paint, sanding between coats with a #320-grit sanding sponge.

With the stool's construction complete, you only have to wait for nature to take its course. One night while you are lying in bed you'll hear a sharp crack or pop – it's the sound of your stool's seat splitting and becoming historically accurate.

The 1" × 3" grip for the stool is a little tight for most adult hands, but it looks right. You might consider making it a little bigger if you have big mitts.

Prairie Spindle Chair

BY DAVID THIEL

Many Arts & Crafts enthusiasts consider the cube chair the stylistic peak of the Arts & Crafts movement. This version borrows heavily from a chair made by the L. & J.G. Stickley company, but the narrow spindles are characteristic of architect Frank Lloyd Wright's designs. Traditional quartersawn white oak and solid construction techniques make it true to Arts & Crafts principles.

Though the chair isn't complicated, there are a lot of repetitive steps in milling the many mortises and tenons. Begin by cutting the lumber to the sizes given in the parts list.

Mortises

There are 82 mortise-and-tenon joints in the chair. A mortiser was my tool of choice, though a plunge router using a $\frac{1}{2}$" straight bit is another option.

Each leg receives two $\frac{1}{2}$" wide × $\frac{7}{8}$" deep × 4" long mortises for the stretchers between the legs. These mortises start 10" up from the bottom of each leg, so this is a good time to determine the legs' orientation, making sure the best quartersawn figure faces out where it can be seen. The $\frac{1}{2}$" wide × $\frac{7}{8}$" deep × $1\frac{1}{2}$" long apron mortises are next. The rear legs receive apron mortises on the same two faces as the stretcher mortises, while the front legs receive only one apron mortise per leg, located on the side facing the back legs. These mortises start $\frac{1}{4}$" down from the top so the aprons will be flush to the leg top.

Once you've completed the leg mortises, move to the side stretchers and aprons and mark each for the $11\frac{1}{2}$" × 1" × $\frac{5}{8}$" deep mortises for the spindles. The mortises nearest the legs should be marked starting $1\frac{1}{4}$" in from each end — a $\frac{3}{4}$" allowance for the stretcher tenon yet to be cut, plus $\frac{3}{4}$" spacing between the leg and the first spindle. Allow a 1" interval between each spindle, and this will provide even spacing.

The back stretcher and apron are marked similarly, but the first mark is made $1\frac{3}{4}$" in from either end and then every inch. Cutting the through-mortises in the arms will be among your final tasks, so you're through with mortises for now.

Tenons

The next step is to make all the tenons. Whichever piece you start with, the stretchers, aprons or slats, the process will be the same steps with just slight dimension adjustments.

I prefer to form the cheeks first and define the shoulder last. This method prevents the saw-kerf from being seen on the shoulder, and prevents a waste piece from being trapped by the blade where it can be thrown back at you. In our case, the waste on most pieces is all sawdust, so there's less risk of throwback, but it's still a good thing to be aware of.

I started with the spindles and set my rip fence for about $\frac{5}{8}$" and the blade height for $\frac{7}{16}$". By running the spindle through with one face against the fence, then turning it and running the opposite face against the fence, I was certain my tenon would be centered.

When the setup was a good fit for the mortise, I attached a guide block to my miter gauge to keep my fingers away from the blade while making sure the slat didn't wobble during the cut. Two passes on each end of each spindle, and I was ready to cut the tenons to width. I readjusted my simple miter gauge jig and completed the cuts.

The final cut on the tenons defines the shoulder of the $\frac{1}{2}$"-long tenons. The shoulder depth is cut using a stop block clamped onto the miter gauge as shown. Again, two passes are made on each end, then the blade depth is reset and the width passes are made. These same steps are used to form the tenons on the stretchers and aprons.

The through-tenons on the front legs are made last. Again, the same three steps are used, with the final tenon size being $1\frac{1}{2}$" × $1\frac{1}{2}$" × 1". Before you begin

A bench-top mortiser makes the repetitive work more manageable.

Time spent carefully laying out the mortise locations will pay big dividends during assembly.

A featherboard provides stability and safety while cutting the tenons.

A simple setup on the miter gauge makes cutting the tenons consistent.

Use a simple stop block clamped onto the miter gauge to set the tenon shoulder depth.

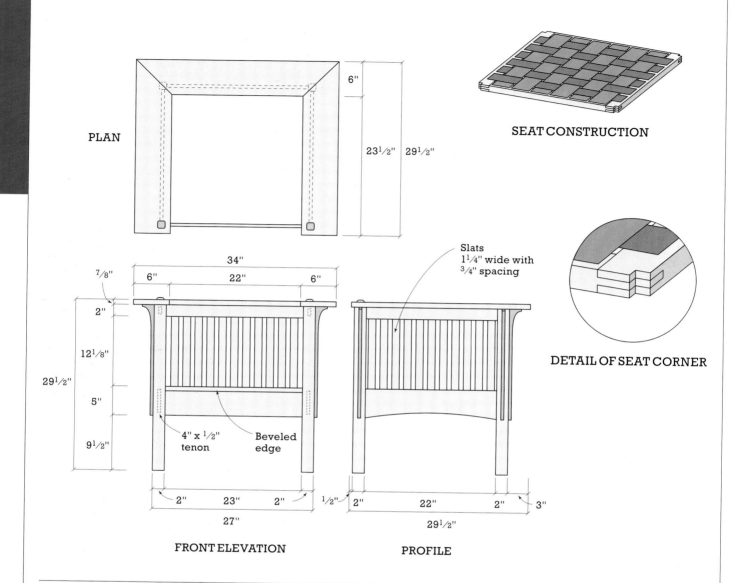

PLAN

SEAT CONSTRUCTION

DETAIL OF SEAT CORNER

Slats
1¹/₄" wide with
³/₄" spacing

FRONT ELEVATION

PROFILE

4" x ¹/₂" tenon

Beveled edge

Prairie Spindle Chair

LET.	NO.	ITEM	T	W	L	MATERIAL	COMMENTS
			DIMENSIONS (INCHES)				
A	2	Front legs	2	2	29⁵/₈	White oak	
B	2	Rear legs	2	2	28⁵/₈	White oak	
C	2	Arms	⁷/₈	6	29¹/₂	White oak	Miters, one end
D	1	Back top	⁷/₈	6	34	White oak	Miters, both ends
E	2	Front & back stretchers	³/₄	5	24¹/₂	White oak	TBE
F	2	Side stretchers	³/₄	5	23¹/₂	White oak	TBE
G	2	Side aprons	³/₄	2	23¹/₂	White oak	TBE
H	1	Back apron	³/₄	2	24¹/₂	White oak	TBE
I	33	Spindles	⁵/₈	1¹/₄	13¹/₈	White oak	TBE
J	6	Corbels	³/₄	2¹/₂	19	White oak	
K	22	Pegs		¹/₈	2	White oak	Dowels
L	4	Seat cleats	1	1	22	Poplar	
M	2	Seat frame pieces	³/₄	2	24	Poplar	Bridle joint, both ends
N	2	Seat frame pieces	³/₄	2	23	Poplar	Bridle joint, both ends
TBE = tenons, both ends							

The side assemblies should fit snugly, but if you force them, you'll split the wood!

When attaching the legs to the side assembly, the best grain should face outward.

When drilling the peg holes, a piece of tape on the drill bit provides an inexpensive depth gauge.

Keep the saw blade parallel to the leg surface while cutting the peg flush.

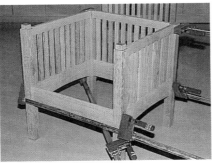

Clamp diagonally across the chair frame, to adjust square to perfect.

Gluing on the corbels is fairly simple, but watch for glue squeeze-out.

sanding, cut the profile on the corbels, or arm supports, and cut the arch on the bottom of the side stretchers. A scaled template for the corbels is provided on page 58. I used a band saw to make the cuts wide of the pencil lines, then I sanded many of the saw marks out with a sanding drum chucked into my drill press. Final sanding for the curved edges is done with a random orbit sander.

Another detail prior to sanding is the 45° bevel on the top front edge of the front stretcher. This attractive detail will keep your legs from going to sleep! I made the cut on the table saw, leaving a ³⁄₈" face on the top edge.

With the sanding done, you're ready to assemble. Start with one set of side aprons and stretchers and 11 slats. Test the tenon fits for any problems, and use a chisel to adjust the fit if necessary. To assemble the side, I clamped the stretcher into my front bench vise and applied glue to all the mortises. Make sure you use enough glue, but remember that too much may keep the tenon from seating all the way in. My tenon fit was tight enough to require just a little persuasion

What is Quartersawing?

Quartersawing is the practice of first cutting a log into quarters and then cutting the resulting pie-shaped wedges into boards. When a quartersawn board is examined from the end, the annular rings will run 45° to 90° to the face. This results in a board with extraordinary stability. Boards with ring angles between 45° and 80° are known as rift cuts and angles between 80° and 90° are fully quartersawn.

Quartersawn oak was, and still is, the wood of choice for Stickley pieces. When quarter-sawn, its medullary rays (tissues radiating from the pith of a tree trunk that intersect the growth rings and carry sap) yield a very unique decorative pattern with exposed rays known as flakes.

Quartersawn oak has near vertical end grain.

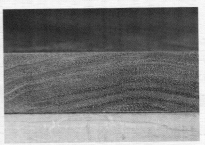

Flat cut wood has less than 45° end grain.

with a dead-blow hammer, but if your tenons require more than a friendly tap, you risk bulging out the thin, 1/8" sides of the mortise.

After all the tenons are seated in the stretcher, remove the piece from the vise and place the apron in the same position, and insert the slat tenons into the apron mortises.

Next, dry-fit the tenons of the assembled side into the mortises on the front and back legs. When the fit is good, glue the mortises, assemble and clamp.

Doweling the Joints

While the sides dry, drill the legs for pinning the tenons and then insert the pegs. Use masking tape to mark the 1/8" drill bit at a depth of 1½" and drill two holes at each stretcher tenon and one hole at each apron tenon.

A flush-cutting bit makes clean work of the through-mortise in the arms.

Cut the oak pegs to 2" lengths and then sand a chamfer on one end to allow it to slip into the hole easily. After putting a small amount of glue into the peg hole, tap the peg home, making sure the peg's end grain runs opposite the grain of the leg.

A Square Chair

After the sides are dry, use the same procedure to assemble the rear slat assembly. Then glue it and the front stretcher between the sides and clamp. You should also check for square at this time, using a clamp to adjust. If your clamps allow it, the corbels can be glued in place at this time. If you've got clamps in the way, wait till the glue on the chair frame is dry and then glue the corbels in place. It's important to center the corbel on the leg and

keep the top flush with the leg top on the back leg and the tenon shoulder on the front leg.

Through-Mortises in the Arms

Next cut the through-mortises using the router template shown below. Use a table saw to make the template, and simply tack some 3/4" × 3/4" strips to the underside as indexing guides. These guides provide correct mortise placement, while allowing you to use only one clamp to hold the template in place during routing.

Once the template is ready, fit it over one of the arms and mark the location of the mortises. Unless you want to make two templates, you'll have to work from the underside of one of the arms, so pay attention to which side displays the best figure.

Use a 1⅛" boring bit chucked into the drill press to clear away most of the waste from the hole, then rout, and square out the mortises' corners using a chisel.

The 45° miter joints at the back corners of the arms are then glued together

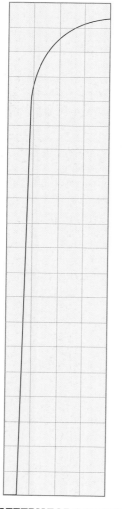

PATTERN FOR CORBELS
Each square = ½"

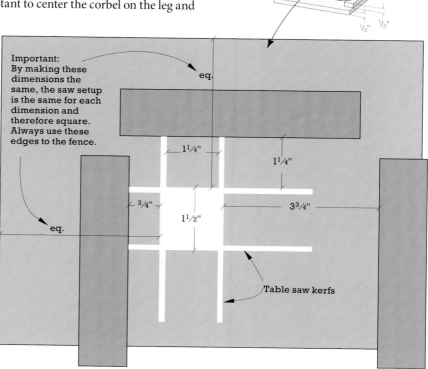

Important:
By making these dimensions the same, the saw setup is the same for each dimension and therefore square. Always use these edges to the fence.

eq.

eq.

1¼"

1¼"

3/4"

3¾"

1½"

Table saw kerfs

½" ½"

Gluing the arms in place is another chance to adjust the chair for square.

using biscuits to align and strengthen the joint. But before gluing, gently tap the arms into place over the tenons and mark the height of the arm on the tenon with a pencil. Then carefully remove the arms, and use a biscuit joiner and glue to fasten the mitered arm pieces together.

While these dry, bevel the top of the leg tenon by marking a square centered $^3/_8$" in around the top of the tenon, then use a random orbit sander to form a chamfer around the top of the tenon. This gives the chair an elegant finishing touch.

Final Assembly

Once the arm assembly dries, apply glue to the entire top edge of the chair aprons and corbels and place the arms over the tenons.

To finish the piece in an appropriate style for an Arts & Crafts piece, apply a brown aniline dye to the raw wood, then spray on a coat of lacquer, or shellac. When that has dried, apply a warm brown glaze, wiping off the excess until you have achieved a uniform color. After allowing the glaze to dry overnight, apply finishing coats of lacquer or orange shellac for a very warm color.

We went to an upholsterer for the seat, using a simple foam cushion mounted on a flat poplar frame. The sizes for the frame are given in the Schedule of Materials. The seat is then simply dropped onto four cleats mounted to the inside of the chair frame. We also had the upholsterer work up a back cushion at the same time.

After that, the chair is ready to put to important work. Ease down, get comfortable and read *Popular Woodworking* while you plan your next project.

Making the Cushions

If you're like most woodworkers, you use a needle only for splinter removal. So unless you're lucky enough to know a seamstress who can make the chair cushions, you'll need the services of an upholsterer.

My upholsterer recommended a web seat, as shown, with a 3"- to 4"-thick foam cushion. He suggested 1$^1/_2$ yards of fabric that I provided, and he provided the batting and webbing material that was mounted to the frame (that I made using bridle joints at the corners for strength). I had allowed a $^1/_8$" space around the frame (for padding and material). The photos below document the assembly of both the seat and back cushions, if you'd like to tackle the process yourself.

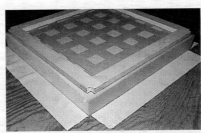

The seat cushion is shown upside down. Rubber webbing has been stapled in place on the frame. Strips of muslin have been glued to foam, which is 1" larger than the frame size.

The muslin has been pulled and stapled in place on the frame bottom. Begin pulling and fastening from the center of each side, then work toward the corners for consistency.

Right side up, the foam is formed by pulling and fastening muslin to give the cushion its final shape.

The upholstery fabric is stapled in place using the same method as the muslin. A layer of fiberfill is simply placed between the foam and fabric to give the cushion loft and smooth and irregularities. Fit the fabric in the corners neatly.

The back cushion is rectangular cut foam wrapped with fiberfill.

The zippered back fabric is sewn with separate end pieces to give it the proper angled shape of a bolster.

Willow Chair

BY CHRISTOPHER SCHWARZ & MICHELLE TAUTE

Building rustic furniture is so unbelievably easy and quick that it's almost unfair to call it woodworking. With just a few tools you can build a bent willow chair in a long afternoon. Smaller projects, such as our magazine rack, can be finished before lunch. And, as if it weren't easy enough already, a remarkably simple new tool has come to market that makes these gypsy chairs sturdier and even faster to build.

In fact, the greatest obstacle in building these chairs is finding the right materials. Luckily, willow trees grow in every state in the continental United States. They thrive near water and are easy to spot along the roadsides in ditches.

In fact, they thrive almost too well. Many arborists consider them nuisance trees. Their roots clog sewer and water lines, and their offspring sprout easily and spread like kudzu. As a result, most people we asked were more than happy to have us lop off a few branches. We got weeping willow branches (*Salix babylonica*), which are great for the bent arms and back, from a willow on a university campus. We got black willow (*Salix nigra*) from a local park after talking to the park board. (If you can't find willow, poplar branches also work.)

With a little effort, you'll soon have more sources for willow than you need. By the way, winter is the perfect time to harvest willow because most of the underbrush around the trees will be dormant and the sap is at rest, meaning the bark won't peel off the branches as they dry.

An Easy Harvest

Luckily you don't need a chainsaw to harvest willow for chairs or small projects. We used a folding pruning saw and a ratcheting hand pruner to cut our branches. Basically you are looking for three different kinds of thicknesses. Branches that are 2" in diameter are great for the frame of the chair. Branches that are ¾" in diameter are perfect for the bent sections of your chair. And small branches, those ⅜" and smaller, are good for decorative trim.

You can build the seat several ways. You can nail really long flexible limbers to the seat rungs and bend them up to also serve as the back. Or you can use 22"

It isn't often that a woodworker gets to play lumberjack. When you're clear-cutting the trees, cut near the base of the tree, as soon as the trunk starts to straighten out. The smaller branches can be cut with the saw or removed with a ratchet pruner.

You can find pruning saws and hand pruners at any home center store, but you'll get better quality at a lower price through gardening catalogs.

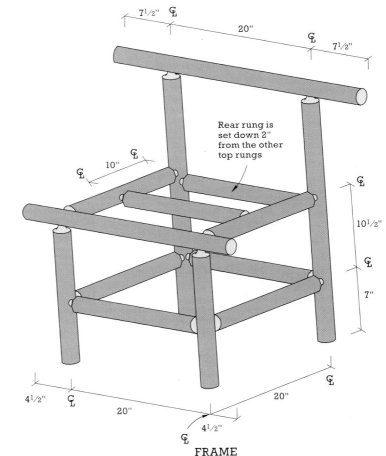

Rear rung is set down 2" from the other top rungs

FRAME

Willow Chair Frame

NO.	ITEM	DIMENSIONS (INCHES) D	L	MATERIAL
2	Back legs	2	30	Willow
2	Front legs	2	17	Willow
8	Rungs	2	20	Willow
1	Front rung	2	29	Willow
1	Top rung	2	35	Willow

We kept our "limbers" in a five-gallon bucket filled with water. You can make your bendable limbs even more limber by first standing on the thick end and pulling the rest of the limb up toward you. Then take a step forward on the limb and pull it up again. Repeat the process most of the way up the limb. Don't pull too hard, or the limb will snap.

To cut the tenons with the power tenon cutter, clamp your rung to a table or your workbench, keeping it as level as possible. Start the cut slowly to make sure your drill is centered on the rung. Then fire away.

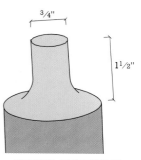

DETAIL OF TENON STUB

Handscrews are the best way to hold your legs level while you drill the mortises. Mark the location of the mortise with a scratch awl. Then drill the mortise. I used a piece of tape on the Forstner bit to gauge how deeply I should drill.

lengths spaced 1" apart for the seat, and then nail longer lengths between the seat pieces for the back. Finally, nail a 23½"-long stick to the front of all the ends of the seat's sticks to protect the undersides of your knees. We also add little trim pieces made from willow scraps. The little design on the front of our chair was made from six sticks that were each 20" long.

Here's the best part – you're done. No sanding, no staining, no finishing. The best way to finish one of these chairs is to buy a seat cushion, set the chair outside and let Mother Nature do her job.

Store Your Harvest

Once you've gathered your branches, you need to separate them into two piles. The thicker branches need to dry in the sun for a week or so, while you need to keep the bendable limbs – we call them "limbers" – in a bucket of water so they remain flexible.

We used the driest branches for the chair's rungs, and we used branches that were a little wetter for the four legs. There's a good reason for this. All of the rungs will have tenons cut on the ends (this is where the new tool will come in handy), while your legs will house the mortises. As wood dries it shrinks, so if your four legs are a little wetter, they will tighten more around the drier rungs, making a very stiff, and natural, joint.

Keep in mind that this isn't rocket science, so don't get too haired over if your moisture content isn't perfect. After a couple weeks, most of our branches had a moisture content of about 15 percent, which is dry enough.

Cut Your Tenons

First cut all your pieces to size and square the ends the best you can. Now cut the tenons on both ends of the eight chair rungs. You could whittle the tenons using a knife, but there's a new tool on the market that makes this process child's play. The Veritas Power Tenon Cutter chucks into your hand drill and cuts perfect tenons on wet branches. The tenon cutters are pricey, but they are worth every penny. (They are available in three sizes, but we used the ¾" cutter [$92, leevalley.com] for the entire project.

The tenons are ¾" long (plus the shoulder) and ¾" thick. It's tempting to use your cordless drill with the power tenon cutter to make the tenons, but I recommend using an old-fashioned corded drill. Even our professional-quality cordless drills had some trouble making the cuts, and the process drained their batteries quickly.

Even Faster Mortises

Because your tenons are perfectly round and perfectly sized, cutting the mortises is a snap. We used a ¾" Forstner bit in our drill press. If you don't have a drill press, you also could use your hand drill. Just try to make the hole as straight as possible. The wood will bend to some degree to help you, but there are limits. Once you have cut the mortises, you can begin to assemble your chair's frame. We used polyurethane glue in the mortises because it works with wood that has a moisture content up to 20 percent – perfect for this application. Once you insert the tenon into the mortise, secure the joint with a galvanized 1½" brad. Once this frame is assembled, allow it to dry overnight. When dry, clean the glue squeeze-out with a chisel.

Nail the Limbers

Once you've limbered up your limbers, it's time to nail them in place. The arms are about 53" long. You might want to leave them even longer and cut them to size after attaching them to the seat's frame. I cut a small notch with a chisel in each of the eight arm pieces at the point where the arm meets the top rung. This makes the joint stronger. Nail or screw the first arm piece to the area under the overhang of the top rung. Put the first arm piece next to the leg. Then bend the piece around the frame and nail it to the bottom front rung. Add as many arm pieces as will fit.

The Back

Save your best and longest pieces for the back. I recommend making a plywood template for this (an idea I borrowed from the book *Making Bent Willow Furniture* by Brenda and Brian Cameron, from Storey Books). The template requires a piece of ³⁄₄" plywood measuring 27" × 19". The idea is to make one end of the plywood into a half-circle shape with a radius of 13¹⁄₂". You could mark this radius using trammel points or a piece of string 13¹⁄₂" long. Cut the shape with a jigsaw or band saw. Notch the ends so the template fits over the arms as shown in the photo.

Now nail in your first back piece. Nail one end to the stretcher on the frame's side, then bend it outside the arm pieces and over the template to the other side of the frame. Nail it in place. You might have to splice two shorter pieces together to reach the optimum 112" length. Repeat this process with four more limbs.

Cut a notch in the arm pieces here

Notch the template over the arms

Nail this 23¹⁄₂"-long twig to cover the ends of the seat's sticks

The trick to getting these limbers to bend together is to cut off the little knots and imperfections with a pocket knife. Then put as many nails as possible into the sticks to hold them in place.

Here you can see the back halfway finished. The plywood template makes this step quick and easy.

Shaker-Style Rocker

BY OWEN REIN

Most woodworkers don't list a hatchet as part of their tools, but when I'm chopping out the shape for the top slat it's my best friend.

The first thing to say about making chairs is they are hard to do. Chairs need to be strong because they get moved around a lot. There isn't always a lot of wood thickness to make the joints, and if you don't get them right, sooner or later the chair will break or fall apart. Aside from the structural demands, comfortable chairs need to conform to and support the human body in a balanced posture. Having taken care of all this, good chairs should be attractive because they stick out into a room and generally get looked at a lot.

Chairs don't design well on paper, especially post and rung chairs. The critical elements that make a well-balanced chair can't really be understood until you've sat on what you've made. For this reason I usually start my students off by suggesting that they plan on making half a dozen chairs rather than expecting to get everything right the first time. There are curves and bends that I don't even measure; I just know what feels good and where it should go. This comes only with practice.

I made my first rocking chair about 18 years ago working from measured drawings from the rocking chairs at Mt. Lebanon's Shaker community. I was not at all pleased with the way my first chair sat. So, through a process of trial and error that lasted about four years, I finally got to a point where I was well pleased.

If I haven't scared you off, and you would still like to try your hand at making a good rocking chair, I'll give you my best advice and the necessary information on how to make one of my Shaker-style rocking chairs.

Selecting the Wood

For the necessary strength in a chair, I use hardwoods with a good straight grain – white oak, hickory and sometimes ash. Maple would make a nice chair but it doesn't grow well here in Arkansas. The size of the growth rings matters, too. Slow growth wood is weak and brittle, and wood that grows too fast is sometimes hard to work and has a greater tendency to warp and check while drying. Because of this I don't like to use wood that has growth rings much smaller than $1/16$", or larger than $3/16$".

I always make my chair pieces from green wood and let them season before they are assembled. Along with other advantages in this process, it's important to assemble the chairs while the wood in the legs is a little green, but the spokes should be very dry. If done right the joints shrink tight and the spokes won't ever come loose. If green wood isn't convenient, dried wood can be used if properly glued.

Making the Pieces

I split out my green pieces from the log and shape them with a drawknife. If this is too rustic for you, you could use a table saw to cut pieces from milled lumber and shape the pieces on a lathe.

I start by making the back legs, starting with $1 5/8$" square by 48"-long stock, tapering the square pieces on the inside and front faces. Orient front and back on the legs so that the growth rings run side-to-side, not front-to-back. Start the taper 20" up from the bottom and end with the top at $1 1/8$" square. Then bevel the edges on the whole leg so that it is an even octagon in cross-section (this brings you halfway to being round, but still leaves you with sides).

Make the front legs about 24" long and $1 5/8$" square with the edges beveled to also form an octagonal shape.

Now prepare all the spokes. If you're working green wood, make the spokes longer than necessary and trim them to length later. The front seat spoke and the top and bottom spoke for the back need to be the thickest, about $1 1/8$" in diameter. The other seat spokes can be from 1" to $7/8$", with the rest of the spokes finishing not less than $3/4$" in diameter. All these pieces have their long edges beveled to an octagon shape.

The jigs I use are fairly simple 2× material with blocks added to space and shape the pieces. Two sets of back rails are shown. The jigs for the back legs are even simpler.

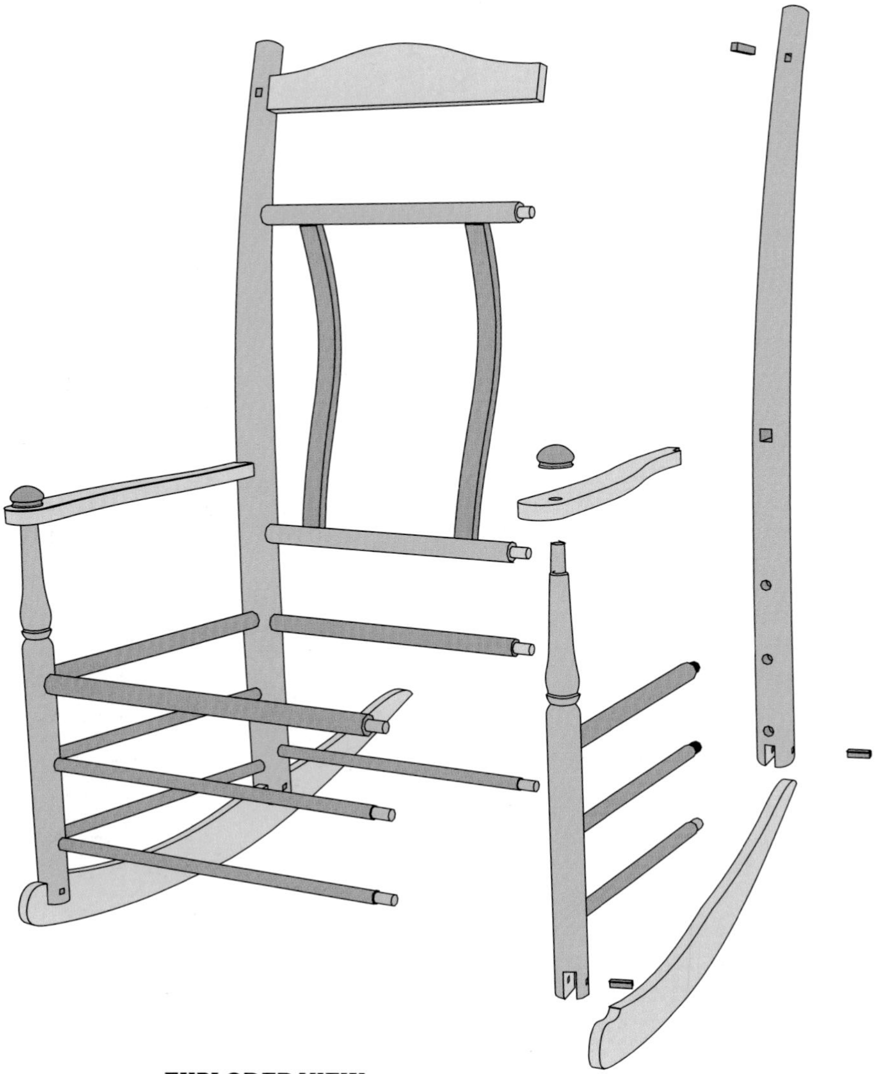

EXPLODED VIEW

Care should be taken when making the two side rails for the back because they will receive a compound bend. Make these two pieces about 5⁄6" × 1 1⁄8" × 26". The extra length helps during bending. The growth rings should run parallel to the width (which will end up being the front and back faces of the rails). Selecting the wood for pieces that will be bent is important. The grain should be clear and straight with no small growth rings. Bevel these as octagons as well.

The two back legs and the two side rails for the back are put in the bending jigs right after I make them. The green wood bends easily and I don't need to do any preparation other than follow the grain and keep the dimensions even. The back legs are placed in the bending jig so the growth rings are perpendicular to the sides. The top of the legs are bent back about 5"–6". Use the scaled diagram to lay out and build a jig for the back side rails.

I mark the date on the pieces after they're in the jigs and set them aside for a month. Even after this time, the wood will be green enough to contract on the tenons and form a solid joint. If you use milled lumber, I would suggest steaming the pieces to be bent for about 20 minutes before putting them into the jigs.

Now turn to the other pieces. Cut the arms, the top slat and the two rockers. Again use the templates to shape the rockers and the top slat.

Shaker-Style Rocker

NO.	ITEM	DIMENSIONS (INCHES) T	W	L	MATERIAL
2	Back legs	1 5⁄8 dia.		48	White oak
2	Front legs	1 5⁄8 dia.		24	White oak
1	Seat front spoke	1 1⁄8 dia.		22	White oak
2	Seat side spokes	1 dia.		18	White oak
1	Seat back spoke	1 dia.		18	White oak
2	Front spokes	3⁄4 dia.		22	White oak
5	Side and rear spokes	3⁄4 dia.		18	White oak
2	Back top & bottom spokes	1 1⁄8 dia.		18	White oak
2	Back side rails	5⁄8	1 1⁄8	26	White oak
2	Arms	3⁄4	4	20	White oak
1	Top slat	3⁄8	3 1⁄2	18	White oak
2	Rockers	5⁄8	5	34	White oak
2	Cookies		1 3⁄4 dia.		Walnut

Dimensions are rough-shaped sizes and include tenon.

The tenon on each of the spokes includes a "locking ring." The depression cut around the circumference of the tenon allows the wood from the leg to expand into the ring as it dries, locking the tenon in place.

Making the Joints & Assembling the Frame

Start by taking the two extra thick spokes for the back (H) and taper the ends starting about $2\frac{1}{2}$" from the end down until the end is a little more than $\frac{5}{8}$" (this is done so the thick spokes will be more graceful where they meet the back legs).

Next, cut a $\frac{5}{8}$"-round tenon on both ends of each of the other spokes. On all but one of the spokes these tenons are 1" long. The top spoke for the back panel has $\frac{3}{4}$"-long tenons to accommodate the taper in the back legs. Chamfer the ends of the tenons, bevel the shoulders and cut a "locking ring" (see photo) around the middle of the tenon. My favorite way of cutting these tenons is on a foot-operated reciprocating lathe.

Fitting the back together is tricky and needs to be done carefully because the joints are small and there isn't a lot of wood to work with.

First, drill $\frac{1}{2}$" centered holes 4" from each end in the bottom spoke. Drill the holes as deep as you can without poking through the other side. With a $\frac{1}{4}$" mortising chisel, cut out the corners and make the hole square (this is done to help keep the side rails from twisting).

Take the side rails out of the bending jig. Adjust the curves to match and trim the tops if necessary. Measuring down from the tops, cut the rails to $19\frac{1}{2}$" long. Cut square tenons on the bottom end of each rail to fit the mortises cut into the

bottom spoke. Mark each side rail and each mortise so that you will know which goes where.

Repeat this process with the top spoke and the top ends of the side rails, drilling the mortises in the top rail $3\frac{1}{2}$" from the ends.

After the joints are made I round off all the spokes with a half-round spokeshave. The side rails I round off with a carving knife. With the seat spokes and the back it is important to do a good job rounding the pieces because sharp corners will cause increased wear on the weaving. I taper the spokes that go below the seat slightly towards the ends, leaving small, even shoulders.

With my carving knife I flatten the sides of each round tenon perpendicular to the growth rings. When the spokes are driven into the holes drilled in the legs, they are positioned so that these flats run up and down, so that the round parts of the tenon exert most of the pressure toward the top and bottom of the leg, to avoid splitting the leg. Lastly, all the spokes that will be exposed are rubbed down with a handful of shavings to burnish the spokes.

Now take the two front legs and trim their bottoms flat. At this point I rough out the vase turning that goes above the seat. Mark 15" up from the bottom and cut a $\frac{1}{4}$"-deep saw cut all the way around the leg. While holding the leg in a drawhorse, I use a push knife to carve a valley about 1" wide with the saw cut at the bottom of the valley. Next, I use a drawknife to taper the top end of the leg down to about $\frac{7}{8}$", trying to leave a pleasing "bulb" look above the valley.

Decide which leg will go on which side of the chair. Then, with the legs side by side, orient the grain so that the growth rings are at an angle to each other (not parallel or perpendicular) and the youngest growth rings are on the outside corners where the seat will be. This is done to help prevent splitting.

Measure up from the bottom $12\frac{1}{2}$" and make a mark for the top (seat) spoke. The middle spoke goes at 8" up from the bottom. The bottom spoke goes at $3\frac{1}{2}$" up from the bottom.

Cut the top off the leg about 23" up from the bottom, and for a $\frac{5}{8}$" round tenon about $1\frac{1}{2}$" long with a beveled

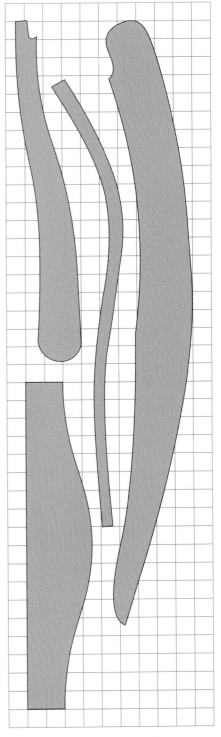

PARTS PATTERNS
Each square = 1"

shoulder. Chamfer the end, but don't flatten the sides.

Take the back legs out of their jig, adjust the bends to match if necessary, then trim their bottoms. On the insides of the legs measure up from the bottom and put a mark at 11" for the seat spoke. The bottom spoke goes at 3⅛" up from the bottom. The bottom spoke of the back panel goes 5½" above the seat at 16½" up from the bottom. Don't mark for the top of the back panel. The center of the mortise for the top slat is at 42" up from the bottom. Here I chop out the 2"-long mortise for the top slat with a ¼" mortise chisel, cleaning up the sides with a 1" flat chisel. Make the mortise deep and square and straight, without going through the side of the leg.

To determine the proper drilling depth for the spokes in the legs, I use an adhesive bandage wrapped around the base of the drill bit as a depth stop. I use a drilling shelf to keep things straight (see photo), though I still use my eyeballs to find the center of the leg. Drill ⅝" holes as deep as you can for all the spokes. To determine where to drill for the top spoke of the back panel, assemble it without glue and snug the bottom spoke into its hole. I even drill the top spoke hole just a hair low to get a squeezing effect on the back panel assembly.

When all the holes for the front and

While drilling the mortises, holding the legs firmly in place is all important. I use a 6" wooden shelf where the legs are held against a backstop by driving a wedge between the leg and a large wooden peg placed in a 1" hole drilled in the shelf. Scribing a perpendicular line on the shelf keeps the drill bit square with the leg. Keeping the drill bit level with the shelf keeps the holes in line with each other.

back spokes have been drilled (we haven't done anything for the side spokes yet), round off all four legs with the spokeshave, trim the valley of the vase turning with the carving knife, then rub the legs down with wood shavings.

Shape the top slat and fashion tenons on its ends to fit the mortises chiseled in the back legs. Make sure the slat is good and smooth and that all corners are rounded.

Glue and assemble the back, taking a second to look it over for squareness. Put glue in the mortises, but not on the tenons. Likewise, glue and assemble the front and the back of the chair, making sure to keep the flats of the spoke tenons

running parallel to the length of the legs. The tenons should fit tight. A heavy neoprene mallet knocks the pieces together quickly.

Now it's time to drill the holes for the side spokes. The centers for all but two of these holes are drilled ⁹⁄₁₆" above the centers for the back and front spokes. The back holes for the two bottom side spokes go ⁹⁄₁₆" below the bottom back spoke. I do it this way so that I'll have more wood for the rear rocker joint.

These side holes will not be at right angles to the front or rear spokes. Being that the seat is a trapezoid, the front angle will be less than 90 and the rear angle will be greater. A template of the seat makes a good drilling guide.

I drill the side holes the same way I do the front and back holes. The only difference is that this time when I put the leg on the drilling shelf, the leg on the other side is sticking up in the air in front of my face. If this is the front leg, I move it toward me 2" before securing the bottom leg. If it is the back leg I push it away from me 2".

When drilling the side holes, also drill ⅝" holes 1" up from the bottom of each leg for the beginning of the rocker joint. The back holes for the rocker joint need to be drilled at an angle to match the top of the rocker pattern. Drill the rocker joint holes all the way through the legs. Also, this is when to drill the holes in the back legs where the back end of the arm will go.

Glue and assemble, and there you have the basic frame. Eyeball the frame and if it's out of whack, you can usually

Drying Green Spokes

As mentioned earlier, using a combination of dried wood and green wood improves joint strength. While air-drying works well with the legs, to have the spokes dry enough to be captured by the shrinking green wood of the legs, they must be dried further. But it's important to dry the spokes correctly to avoid splitting, warping and checking.

In my shop, the spokes are stacked up on my counter so that each spoke will get plenty of air circulation around it. After the spokes have air dried like this for a month or more I take them home and bake them in the oven to get them "kiln" dried. With the spokes spaced out on the oven shelves, I set the dial on warm (my oven door naturally stays ajar without a 2×4 against it). The oven is left on for a few hours and then turned off for a few hours. This cycle is repeated several times and sometimes I even leave the oven on overnight.

Spokes are easy to dry and there are lots of ways of doing it. In previous houses I stored the spokes in the space above the water heater and in a box on top of a gas refrigerator where I kept the air-dried spokes for a week. The key to drying spokes is to do it slowly, in stages, with lower temperatures and lots of air movement.

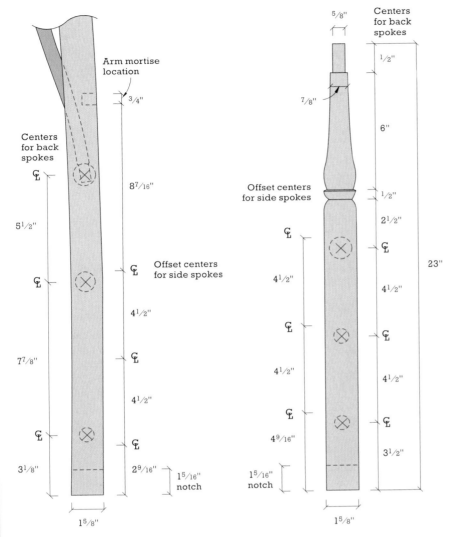

BACK LEG PROFILE

Arm mortise location

Centers for back spokes

Offset centers for side spokes

3/4"

8 7/16"

5 1/2"

4 1/2"

7 7/8"

4 1/2"

3 1/8"

2 9/16"

1 5/16" notch

1 5/8"

FRONT LEG PROFILE

5/8"

Centers for back spokes

7/8"

Offset centers for side spokes

1/2"

6"

1/2"

2 1/2"

4 1/2"

4 1/2"

4 1/2"

3 1/2"

23"

4 9/16"

1 5/16" notch

1 5/8"

---

the tenon. Check the depth of the hole in the cookie, then trim the top of the tenon if it is too long.

Remove the arm and make a saw cut to form the wedged tenon in the front leg. Make the cut perpendicular to the side spokes and cut down past the mark that you made earlier by about 1/8" or so.

Now, out of some dry hardwood, make a wedge to fit this slot. Make sure it isn't too long or it'll hang up the cookie, not too thick or it may split the cookie, and not too thin or it won't spread the tenon enough to keep everything together tight.

Glue the mortises, assemble the arm with the wedge in place, then carefully drive the cookie home with the mallet. As the cookie covers the tenon it will force the wedge in place.

Scrape or whittle off any unsightly marks and put a coat of finish on the frame. I like using 100 percent tung oil (make sure it says this on the label). It is non-toxic and can be left to soak in overnight before being rubbed down. Also this kind of finish is very easy to maintain.

Weaving the Seat

To weave the seat and back on my rocking chairs I use hickory bark or Shaker tape. I usually weave a two-twill herringbone pattern, or a variation thereof.

The procedure for weaving most materials is about the same. The warp

---

improve the situation by pushing on the frame or using a rope and turn buckle.

Completing the Frame

The sides of the rocker joints are cut with a handsaw. The corners are then squared with the 1/4" mortising chisel, and the sides are trimmed with a carving knife. Use a scrap piece of 5/8" board to check the fit and alignment front to back. The fit should be snug without splitting the joint.

Next square up the mortises in the back legs for the arms with a 1/4" mortising chisel. This keeps the arms from twisting.

Now drill 5/16" holes and peg the top slat. I carve square-headed pegs out of walnut. Then cut the top of the back legs off where they look good and trim the ends with the carving knife.

Fitting the Arm

On one of the arm blanks draw the shape of the arm and cut it out. Use this arm as the pattern for the other arm. Drill a 5/8" hole in the front of the arm to receive the tenon on the top of the front leg. Smooth and shape the arm with a drawknife.

Fit the back tenon and bevel all exposed corners of the arm with the carving knife. On the underside of the arm countersink the hole to match the bevel on the shoulder of the front leg tenon.

Assemble the arm dry and mark the tenon at the top surface of the arm. I use a "cookie" to cap the front leg tenon. The cookies are made out of walnut and have a dome shape with a diameter of about 1 3/4". I rough them out on a lathe and finish them off with a carving knife. A 5/8" hole is drilled in the bottom of each to fit

After drilling the starter hole and cutting out the waste, I clean up the rocker notch in the legs with a chisel.

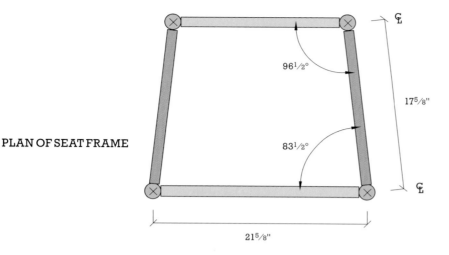

PLAN OF SEAT FRAME

96½°

83½°

17⅝"

21⅝"

is put on first, running front to back. The tension comes from weaving side to side so, to accommodate this, a little bit of slack needs to be cut in the warp. My general rule of thumb is when wrapping the warp, snug up each run without pulling it tight.

Also, never nail anything to the chair. Not only might you split a part of the chair, you might also split that which you want to nail to the chair. There is a much better way. Simply loop the material around the back spoke and tie it, or in the case of Shaker tape, loop it and stitch it.

When weaving the back panel, lay the warp in running top to bottom. Extra slack is needed in the warp to accom-

modate the curve in the back panel. Knowing how much slack to leave takes practice, and if you find that you didn't do the warp right while weaving, I wouldn't be ashamed to start over and do it again.

A few short pieces are added into the weave at the front corners of the seat to fill up the empty places left by the seat's trapezoidal shape.

Making the Rockers

Trace the rocker pattern onto a ⅝" thick board, trying to match the sweep of the rocker and the sweep in the grain. Cut the rockers out with a band saw. With the two rockers held together with a vise or

clamp, finish the edges with a rasp. Pay close attention to the bottom edge, running your hand back and forth along the length of the arc to make sure that there won't be any bumps in the rocker.

Bevel the corners with a carving knife and scrape the surfaces smooth. With the chair upside down, the final fitting of the rockers is done using chisels to make adjustments to the notch.

Glue the rockers in place. While the glue is setting up, cut four ⅜" dowels about 2" long. I split these dowels out of scraps of straight-grain walnut. After roughing out the pieces with the carving knife, I drive them through a dowel reamer (a piece of plate steel with a wallered-out ⅜" hole drilled in it) to get the exact size.

After the glue in the rocker joint is set, drill ⅜" holes and glue the dowels in place. Saw the excess off.

More coats of tung oil go on the frame of the chair, and before I call the chair done I give it one last coat of oil and wet sand the whole frame with #400-grit wet/dry sandpaper. This is the only sanding I do.

Making chairs is a lot different than making tables or cabinets. Accuracy is important in different ways. Good results don't come from a lot of fastidious measuring or planning. Good chairs are born of experience and a well-practiced system.

The arm shown with the wedge in place in the front-leg split tenon, waiting for a cookie. A finished version is shown behind.

At an early part of the weaving process, the herringbone pattern becomes evident.

Morris Chair

BY CHRISTOPHER SCHWARZ

I don't care what they say about dogs, Morris chairs are a man's best friend. The reclining back, wide arms and expansive seat create the perfect place to watch TV, read the Sunday paper or simply contemplate the finer qualities of a beer.

For the last 10 years, I've spent every weekend planted in the original version of this chair, which was built by the Shop of the Crafters in Cincinnati, Ohio, during the heyday of the Arts & Crafts movement. The Shop of the Crafters was founded by German-American businessman Oscar Onken (1858–1948), who ran a successful framing company until he entered the furniture business in 1902, according to Kenneth R. Trapp's history of the company.

Unlike many furniture makers of the day, Onken didn't want to merely copy the Stickleys of the world. Onken produced an unusual line of Arts & Crafts furniture that was influenced more by German and Hungarian designs than the straight-lined Stickley pieces of the day.

In all honesty, a few of Onken's pieces were kind of ugly. Most, however, had a refinement and lightness that rivaled some of the best work of the day.

This Morris chair is an almost exact replica of the one produced by Onken and his company. It differs in only two ways. One, the original chair was constructed using dowels at the major joints. After almost 100 years of use, the front and back rail came loose. This chair is built using pegged mortise-and-tenon joints. Second, I made one change to the

Make the mortises in the legs before you shape the curve near the bottom or make cutouts on the top.

When pattern-routing the curve on the legs, make sure you have the work firmly clamped in place. I have the pattern and leg wedged between two pieces of oak (the pattern is on the underside of the leg). Then the leg itself is clamped to the table. You also could perform this operation on a router table with a starting pin for pattern-routing.

Morris Chair

LET.	NO.	ITEM	DIMENSIONS (INCHES) T	W	L	MATERIAL	COMMENTS
A	2	Front legs	$1^5/8$	$3^3/4$	21	White oak	$1/2$" TOE
B	2	Back legs	$1^5/8$	$2^1/4$	21	White oak	$1/2$" TOE
C	2	Applied sides	$1^5/8$	$1^3/16$	4	White oak	
D	1	Front rail	$3/4$	$4^3/4$	22	White oak	$3/4$" TBE
E	2	Side rails	$3/4$	$4^3/4$	24	White oak	$3/4$" TBE
F	1	Back rail	$7/8$	$4^3/4$	22	White oak	$3/4$" TBE
G	2	Side slats	$1/2$	$7^5/8$	$11^3/8$	White oak	$1/2$" TBE
H	2	Arm build-ups	$7/8$	6	$4^1/2$	White oak	
I	2	Arms	$3/4$	6	$35^1/4$	White oak	
J	2	Cleats	$3/4$	$1^7/8$	$20^1/2$	White oak	
K	1	Back rod	$3/4$	2	$23^5/16$	White oak	
L	2	Seat stiles	$3/4$	$2^1/2$	$23^1/2$	White oak	
M	5	Seat rails	$3/4$	$2^1/2$	17	White oak	$3/4$" TBE
N	2	Back stiles	$3/4$	$1^7/8$	$28^1/4$	White oak	
O	5	Back rails	$3/4$	$1^7/8$	$17^1/2$	White oak	$3/4$" TBE
P	1	Bottom rail	$3/4$	$3^1/4$	$17^1/2$	White oak	$3/4$" TBE
TOE = tenon, one end; TBE = tenon, both ends							

chair frame so that furniture historians of the future will know instantly that this not an original piece. I did this to prevent people from passing off these reproductions as originals.

Though this project might look daunting to you, it can be completed by beginners who have just a few projects under their belt. There are only a few principles to learn here: mortising, tenoning and routing with a plywood template. Plus, I'll share with you exactly how I achieved this finish, which has been something we've been working at for several years.

How to Save Money on Lumber

Begin by choosing the right quartersawn white oak for this project. It requires about 10 board feet of 8/4 and 30 board feet of 4/4 lumber. Quartered white oak can be expensive, from $6 to $12 a board foot. If you live in the Midwest, or will pass near east-central Indiana on a vacation, I recommend you check out Frank Miller Lumber in Union City, Indiana (765-964-3196). The company is a huge supplier of quartersawn oak. As a result, prices are reasonable, about $4 to $6 a board foot. Once you buy your lumber, save the pieces with the most ray flake for the arms, legs, front and sides. To save money, use flat-sawn oak for the seat and the adjustable back.

Mortises: Machine or No Machine?

First cut all your pieces to size according to the cutting list and begin laying out the locations of your mortises using the diagrams. The rule of thumb is that your

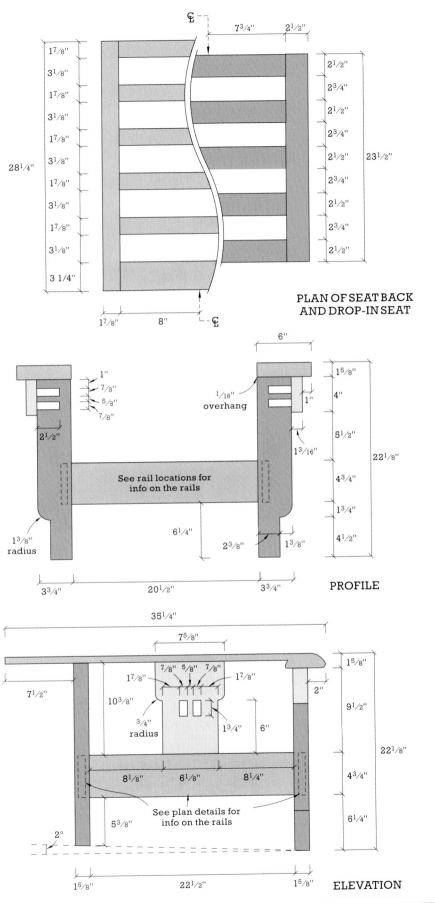

PLAN OF SEAT BACK AND DROP-IN SEAT

PROFILE

ELEVATION

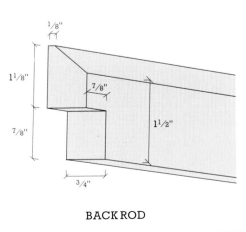

BACK ROD

mortises should be half the thickness of your tenon's stock. When your stock is ¾" thick, your mortises and tenons should be ⅜" thick. That means the tenons for the beefy back rail should be thicker (⁷⁄₁₆") and those for the side slats should be thinner (¼").

Also remember that except for the tenons on the legs and slats, all the tenons are ¾" long. To ensure your tenons don't bottom out in your mortises, it's always a good idea to make your mortises about ¹⁄₁₆" deeper than your tenons are long.

After you mark the locations of all the mortises, it's time to cut them. There are 38 mortises in this project. You'd be nuts to do these all by hand. Use this project as an excuse to purchase a hollow chisel mortising machine (about $325) or a mortising attachment for your drill press (about $70). If you can't swing the cash, I'd make plywood templates and cut the mortises with a router and a pattern bit. Making plywood templates is something covered later in this project.

One more thing: Don't cut the mortises in the arms or the arm buildups until the chair frame is assembled. You'll cut these with a router and a pattern bit after the chair frame is assembled.

Tenons With a Dado Stack

Once you get your mortises cut, make tenons that fit snugly into the mortises.

You can use a tenoning jig or the fence on your table saw, or you can use a router. I prefer to use a dado stack and my miter gauge. See "Climb-Cutting Tenons" for details on how to do this.

While your dado stack is in your saw, cut the groove in the back piece that holds the seat frame. See the drawing for the location of this groove.

Once you cut your tenons, prepare to assemble the drop-in seat and the adjustable back. To save yourself some grief, sand the edges of the rails that you won't be able to get to after the frames are assembled. Now put glue in all the mortises and clamp up the frames. Set them aside to dry.

Climb-Cutting Tenons

I own a commercial tenoning jig for my table saw, but I rarely use it. I get better and faster results by cutting tenons using a dado stack and a trick that professional woodworker Troy Sexton showed me. To avoid tearout on my tenons' shoulders, I "climb cut" the last ¹⁄₁₆" or less of the tenon shoulder. You've probably heard of people climb cutting when using a router. Essentially, it's moving the router in the opposite way you normally would to avoid tearout in tricky grain.

That's exactly what you do on your table saw. The final cut on your shoulders is made by pulling the work toward you over the blade and only tak-

ing a small cut of material. It sounds awkward, but after a few tenons you get used to it. The risk of kickback is minimal because there's no wood trapped between the blade and the fence. To do this safely, hold your work steady and don't get into a hurry.

Here's how you do it: First install a dado stack into your table saw and set the fence for the finished length of your tenon (almost all of the tenons in this project are ¾" long). Set the height of your dado stack to the amount you want to thin one side of your tenon (for most of the tenons in this project, that would be ³⁄₁₆"). Then, using your miter gauge, push the work through the dado stack to cut the majority of your tenon.

When this cut is done, slide the work against the fence and pull the miter gauge back toward you to shave the shoulder of the tenon. Flip the work over and do the other side. Then do the edges.

Set your fence so the dado stack will make a ¾" cut (the length of your tenon). Hold the piece about ¹⁄₁₆" from the fence. Push your work through the blade using your miter gauge.

After you finish that first pass, slide the work against the fence and pull it back toward you over the blade to shave the last little bit of the shoulder.

Repeat the same procedure for the edges of the tenon. (If you like a little more shoulder on your edges, increase the height of the blade.) First push the work forward.

Then slide it against the fence and pull it back toward you to make the final shoulder cut.

Curves & Cutouts

What makes this Morris chair stand out are the curves and cutouts on the legs, arms and slats. Each curve and cutout needs a slightly different strategy.

The large curves on the legs and the small curves on the side slats were cut using a plywood template and a pattern-cutting bit in a router. I made the patterns from ½"-thick Baltic birch plywood. Use the drawings to make your own plywood template using a scroll saw, band saw or coping saw. Smooth all your cuts with sandpaper, then try shaping a couple scraps with your template to make sure your pattern produces the right shape. When satisfied, cut the curves to rough shape on your band saw (about ¹⁄₁₆" shy of your finished line) and clean up the cut with a router and pattern bit. Finish shaping the legs with a chisel.

To produce the large cutouts on the

Peg the tenons that join the front rail to the front legs and the back rail to the back legs. If you've ever pegged tenons before, you know that dowels can be wildly different sizes than they're supposed to be. Here's a trick: If your dowel is a bit undersized, glue it in place and cut it nearly flush to the surface. Then put several drops of thinned glue on the end grain of the dowel. It wicks in the glue, expands and glues up tight. When the glue is dry, cut the dowel flush.

Be sure to make a full-size mock-up of the legs and sides (above) to determine the angle you need to cut on the bottom of the legs. When you determine that angle, use a grease pencil or magic marker to paint the bottom of the legs. I cut the back and front legs simultaneously. Slowly inch your legs in after each cut until all the color is gone (right).

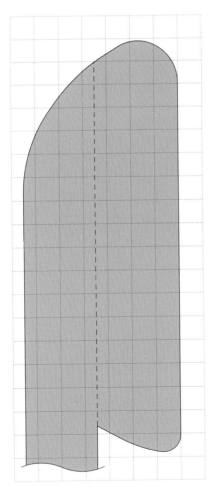

ARM PROFILE

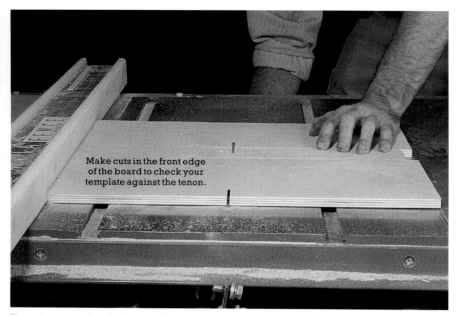

Make cuts in the front edge of the board to check your template against the tenon.

To make a template for the mortises in the arms and the cutouts on the side slats, position your plywood over your table saw and raise the blade into the ply. Move the fence over and repeat. Then turn the pattern 90° and repeat for the other edges of the pattern. Note that I made cuts in the front of the pattern to help me size the pattern to the tenons.

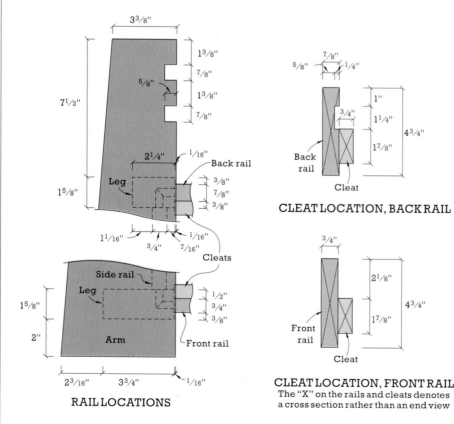

RAIL LOCATIONS

CLEAT LOCATION, BACK RAIL

CLEAT LOCATION, FRONT RAIL
The "X" on the rails and cleats denotes a cross section rather than an end view

front legs, do what Oscar Onken did: Cheat a bit. Make the "cutouts" using a dado stack on your table saw, with the legs on edge. Then glue the applied sides to the legs to cover the open end of the cuts. Instant cutout. While you're at it, cut out the notches on the arm pieces for the rod that adjusts the back.

To complete the legs, you need to cut the bottom of all four legs at a 2° angle so the chair sits flat on the floor. I recommend you make a full-sized mock-up (see photo previous page) so you can get the angle exactly right. Cut the angle on a chop saw.

Assembly

Now you're almost ready to assemble the chair frame. You'll need to first miter the tenons slightly where they meet to fit in the mortises using your table saw. Now finish sand everything. I went to #150 grit using my random-orbit sander and hand sanded the whole piece with #180 grit. Yes, it makes a noticeable difference.

Now glue the front rail between the front legs and the back rail between the back legs. Clamp and allow your glue to dry. Use ¼" dowels to pin the tenons from the inside of the chair. This strengthens the weakest point of this chair. It's at this joint where the original chair came loose.

Glue the side rails between the front and back legs and you can see your chair take shape.

Learn to Make Square Templates

Now you need to work on the arms. First, glue the arm buildup pieces to the front of the arms. Then get ready to cut the mortises on the arms that will hold the tenons on the legs and side slats. A word of advice here. Mock up an arm out of scrap wood and practice on it first.

To make plywood templates for the mortises, you need to make a square hole in the middle of a piece of ply. The best way to do this is by making plunge cuts into your plywood on your table saw. Refer to the photo above that shows how to do this.

Now cut your mortises. I used a template bit with small cutters on the bottom and a guide bearing on top. It's designed for plunging and is called a "mortising bit" in catalogs. If you don't have a bit with these cutters on the bottom, you can still plunge with a standard straight bit that has a guide bearing. Just plunge slowly and wiggle the router a bit as you go. Cut the mortises in two passes.

After you're sure the arms fit on the legs, cut the curve on the front of the arm. Attach the full-size pattern to your arm and cut the shape on a band saw. Clean up the cuts with a stationary belt sander. Now taper the arms with your band saw and clean up the cut with your jointer. Glue the arms and slats in place.

Now shape the back rod that adjusts the seat back angle. Bevel one edge of the rod on your jointer and cut notches on the ends so the rod fits between the arms. Attach the back to the seat frame with a piano hinge. Screw the cleats to the front and back of the frame in the locations shown in the diagram; slip the seat in place.

Finishing

The finish we used requires multiple steps with different finishing products, but the final appearance is worth the trouble. First, dye the chair with a reddish-hued alcohol-based aniline dye. The dye we used is listed in the "Supplies" box. Next, apply one coat of boiled linseed oil (available at any home center store) to the chair. Wipe off the excess oil and allow the finish to dry overnight. The linseed oil seals the wood before your final coloring step and helps bring out the ray flake.

Next, we wiped on a thin coat of glaze made by Behlen's. Wipe the glaze until you achieve an even tone. Allow it to dry overnight. Finally, apply three coats of a clear finish.

Supplies

Rockler Woodworking and Hardware
rockler.com or 800-279-4441

Slotted piano hinge, item #19241, $15.49 for 36"

Woodworker's Supply
woodworker.com or 800-645-9292

J.E. Moser's Medium Red Mahogany alcohol-soluble aniline dye, item #845-772, $14.69 for 1 oz.

Behlen's Van Dyke Shading & Glazing Stain, item #916-759, $28.99 for 1 qt.

Prices as of publication date.

Be sure to make a test arm before you go mortising the real thing. You'll be glad you did.

Inlaid Rocker

BY JIM STACK

When I decided to build an Arts & Crafts rocker, I wanted something a little lighter in looks than most recognized Arts & Crafts pieces. Many of the chairs can look a little chunky and heavy for my taste. This design was produced by the Limbert Furniture Co. of Grand Rapids, Michigan, about 1910. Charles Limbert was a contemporary of Gustav Stickley, but much of his work had a stylized appearance, adding cutouts, sweeps and inlays to separate his work from more austere Arts & Crafts designs.

Design & Layout
First draw a full-scale side and top view of the chair. The drawings help answer questions about construction and what joints to use. They also let you make mistakes that an eraser can correct. I suggest you take the information from the parts list and the diagrams and make your own full-size elevation and plan view drawings.

Building the Legs
Start construction with the legs. The front legs are simple, but remember to orient your wood to show the most attractive face forward. The back legs, with their dog-leg shape, require a routing template. Start by rough-cutting a blank for each leg on the band saw. Next, lay out a $\frac{1}{2}$"-thick plywood template using the dimensions given in the diagrams, then attach it to the blank with flathead screws on the inside of each leg. Put the screws at the mortise locations so the holes won't be seen. Use a router with a template routing bit to shape each leg, and be sure to make one right and one left leg.

Routed Inlays
With the legs shaped to size, lay out the location for the inlays on the front faces of each leg. Start the inlay work by routing the $\frac{1}{8}$"-deep by $\frac{1}{4}$"-wide groove using a straight bit in a plunge router. Next, cut the inlay strips to $\frac{1}{4}$" × $\frac{1}{4}$", to fit a little snug in the width for fitting. This also leaves the inlay proud, to be leveled out once the inlay is glued in place. Walnut works well for the inlay. To glue it in place, put glue into the groove, insert the inlay, and then use a caul and clamps to press the inlay into place. Set these pieces aside to dry for several hours or overnight. After leveling the inlay flush to the leg with a plane, I used a mortiser to create the $\frac{3}{4}$" × $\frac{3}{4}$" square holes to finish the inlay pattern.

Laminated Bending
Now comes the fun part, bending. All the radii are the same, so you have to make only one bending jig for the rockers, arms and back rails. Medium-density fiberboard (MDF) is a stable and affordable material for a bending jig. The longest bent pieces are the rockers, so cut the six $\frac{3}{4}$"-thick jig pieces about 42" long and 8" deep. Next, use a set of trammel points to strike the radius (shown on the diagram) on one of the MDF panels. Rough cut to the outside of the line and then sand to the line. Then use a flush-trim router bit and this first jig part to duplicate the radii on the other five pieces. When the matched layers are placed together, the 4$\frac{1}{2}$" width works well for the arms. Layers can be removed as needed to glue up the narrower parts.

Lamination bending is simply bending thin strips of wood over a form and gluing them together. This is a good way to bend wood because the wood remains stable, the grain patterns of the original face remain when bent, and the final lamination is very strong.

Start the lamination process by cutting pieces for the rockers, arms, and back rails. Cut them $\frac{1}{4}$" wider and longer so you can trim them to size after glue-up. Resaw the blanks into strips a little thicker than $\frac{1}{8}$", keeping the pieces in order as they come off the band saw. Next, drum sand or plane the strips to $\frac{1}{8}$" thick.

Glue Up the Lamination
At glue-up time, have your clamps handy. Be sure to wax or seal all the surfaces on the jig that will come into contact with glue, so the dried glue can be easily removed. With the wood strips in order, apply thinned wood glue to each strip. Then put the whole assembly on the form with a $\frac{1}{2}$"-thick piece of plywood to serve as a caul to even out the clamping pressure. Put the first clamp in the center of the assembly, with the next clamps working out to either end. The clamps should stay in place for *at least* two hours.

Gluing & Cutting the Back Rails
Because the back rails are 3$\frac{1}{2}$" wide, I used only five MDF layers for the bending jig. You'll need seven $\frac{1}{8}$"-thick strips for each of the rails. Apply glue and put the rail assembly in the center of the jig. When the laminations are dry, scrape the glue off one edge and use a jointer to flat-

Start the inlay work on the four legs by using a router with an edge guide to rout the $\frac{1}{4}$"-wide channels for the inlay.

The square ends of the inlays can be done with a mortiser, as shown here, or you can use a router with a template and use a chisel to square out the corners.

ten and square that edge. Then cut the blanks to 3½" wide using the table saw.

Gluing & Cutting the Rockers

The rockers are 2¼" wide, so I left four layers in the jig. I used 10 strips for each rocker. Glue the strips as before, and when dry, square and cut them to width. Next, lay the rockers on the full-size drawings and mark the angles on each end. Cut these angles on the table saw using a miter gauge with a 30" wooden fence attached. Hold the rocker on its side, tight against the fence with the curve arching away from your body. Adjust the miter gauge angle until it matches the angle you want to cut on the end of the rocker. Do this for both ends

of the rockers, then set them aside.

Gluing the Arms

Each arm requires seven ⅛" × 4½" strips, and I used all six layers of the bending form. The arms are radiused only on the back half of the arms, so I clamped to only 13" at one end of the radius form (see top right photo on page 82).

When the arms are dry, scrape the glue off one edge, joint that edge, then cut the blanks to 4¼" wide on the table saw.

Seat Rails & Back Slats

The rails and slats are straight, solid wood pieces. Size them as given in the Schedule of Materials. While you're cut-

ting square wood, also machine cut the seat slats and cleats. The arches on the bottom of the seat rails will be cut after the tenons are cut on the rails.

Mortises & Tenons

As with most solid chairs, the secret to longevity is in the joinery. One of the best possible chair joints is a mortise and tenon. Using the diagrams, lay out the ½" × 5" × 15/16"-long mortises for the seat rails on the front and back legs.

Next cut ½" × 5" × ⅞"-long tenons on both ends of the seat rails. Where the tenons meet at the corner of the leg mortises, you need to cut a 45° bevel on the ends of the tenons.

The back rails are held in place with dowels. To determine the length of the back rails, measure the distance from cheek to cheek on the back seat rail. Then draw a line that same length on a piece of paper. Mark the center, then also mark the center of the back rail. Lay the rail on the paper, and square over from the ends of the line. To cut the curved rails, I laid them (convex side down) against the miter gauge fence. I then put a spacer under the rail, (between the blade and the center point of the rail), to support the rail as the cut is made. This cut is safe as long as you adequately support the rail during the cut. Expect a little tearout on the underside of the cut, so take your cut slowly. Turn the rail and cut the other end the same way. Cut the other rail to match the first.

With the back rails cut to length, it's

Inlaid Rocker

LET.	NO.	ITEM	DIMENSIONS (INCHES)			MATERIAL
			T	W	L	
A	2	Front legs	1¾	1¾	22¼	White oak
B	2	Back legs	1¾	5	36⅝	White oak
C	2	Rockers	1¼	2¼	35¾	White oak
D	2	Seat rails front and back	⅞	6	24¾	White oak
E	2	Side seat rails	⅞	6	20¾	White oak
F	2	Back rails	⅞	3½	23	White oak
G	2	Corbels	⅞	2	8½	White oak
H	2	Seat cleats	⅞	⅞	23	Poplar
J	2	Seat cleats	⅞	⅞	18	Poplar
K	5	Seat slats	⅞	3½	19⅞	Poplar
L	2	Arms	⅞	4¼	24¼	White oak
M	4	Back slats	⅜	3½	16	White oak
N	2	Side slats	⅜	3½	12 5/16	White oak

time to lay out the mortises for the slats
on the upper and lower back rails. Start
by spacing the slats equally along the
rail. Because the rails are curved, and
the tenons are straight, using a fence as a
guide to make the mortises won't work.
Draw $\frac{1}{4}$" × $3\frac{1}{4}$" mortises centered on the
rail, using a 4" wide piece of wood as a
straight edge.

To cut the $\frac{9}{16}$"-deep mortises in the
back rails, I again used the mortiser, but
without a fence, cutting the mortises

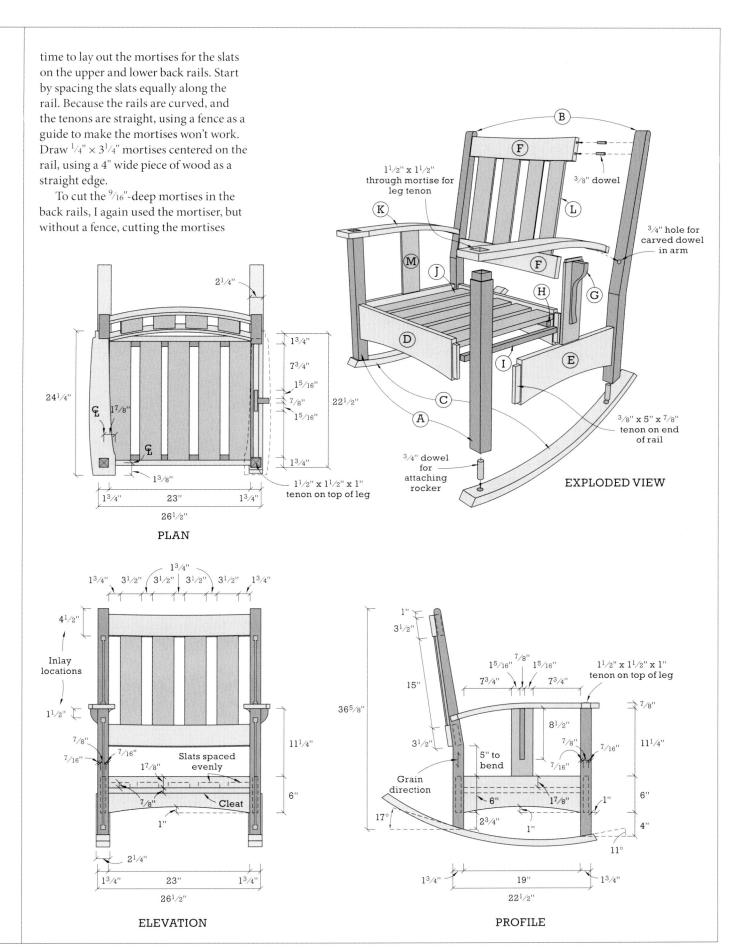

PLAN

ELEVATION

PROFILE

EXPLODED VIEW

$1\frac{1}{2}$" x $1\frac{1}{2}$"
through mortise for
leg tenon

$3\!/8$" dowel

$3\!/4$" hole for
carved dowel
in arm

$3\!/8$" x 5" x $7\!/8$"
tenon on end
of rail

$3\!/4$" dowel
for attaching
rocker

$1\frac{1}{2}$" x $1\frac{1}{2}$" x 1"
tenon on top of leg

In gluing up the laminations, I use a brush to cover every square inch of the wood face. I thin the glue with a little water to make it easier to spread. Thinning will not affect the holding power of the glue. The glue run-out on the sides is a good sign that all surfaces are bonding.

To glue up the arm, the curved end was clamped to the jig while the other half was sandwiched between two straight boards. I found it helpful to glue-up the straight part first, then quickly move the arm to the end of the jig. You may need an assistant to help with this step.

free-hand, following the straight lines as a guide. The mortise needs to be tight, not pretty, as the shoulder of the slat tenon will hide the mortise.

Using the same dimensions as on the back rail mortises, cut the mortises in the two seat side rails for their side slats. Then cut the tenons on all the back slats and just the bottom tenons on the side slats. The tenons on the tops of the side slats will be cut later.

Dry Fitting the Chair
This is a good point to dry-fit the chair and get a look at how it's all going to go together. The two front legs and front seat rail form a subassembly. The two back legs, the back seat rail, the two back rails and the four slats form another sub-assembly. These two subassemblies are joined to one another with the two side seat rails.

While the chair is clamped together dry, put the back rail/back slat assembly in place between the back legs and clamp it with enough pressure to hold it in place. Adjust the fit of the back slat section to its finished position, and mark the top and bottom back rail locations for the dowels.

Doweling the Back Rails
Using the marks made on the back legs, mark the two back rails for two ³⁄₈" dow-

els in each end. It's probably just as easy to drill the dowel locations in the rails free-hand (rather than making a jig) to keep them perpendicular to the end faces of the rails. Then reassemble the back rail/back slat assembly and use dowel centers to locate the dowel locations in the back legs. Use a drill press to drill the holes in the back legs, then put it all back together again to check the fit.

Fitting the Arms
I used a photo in an auction catalog to determine how the arms would fit into the front and back legs. Refer to your working drawings and the diagram of the rear part of the arm to make a full-size paper or cardboard template of the arm. Square over the front of the arms on the table saw, then lay the template square to the front of each arm. Trace the

Use a pattern to trace the layout of the arm. The tenon and wraparound can be made by using the band saw to cut away most of the waste. Use a chisel and file to make the final shape. Check the fit to the back leg as you progress.

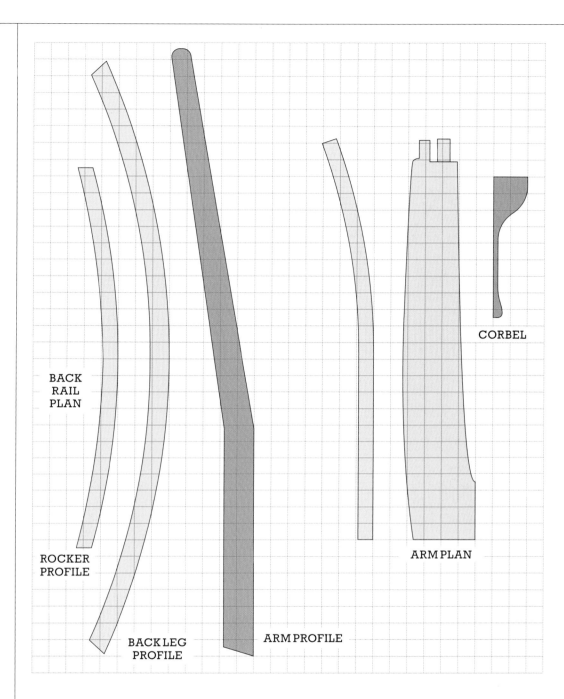

BACK
RAIL
PLAN

ROCKER
PROFILE

BACK LEG
PROFILE

ARM PROFILE

ARM PLAN

CORBEL

SCALED PATTERNS
Each square = 1"

pattern onto the blanks.

Cut out the arms on the band saw leaving the pencil marks, then sand to the pencil marks. Don't cut the tenon and "wraparound" on the back of the arm yet. Instead, just leave the arm about ¹⁄₂" long. By holding the arm blank alongside the front leg and the side of the dry-assembled chair, I was able to mark the arms to length, where they would join the back legs and also draw the angle of the arm at this joint.

With the arm location and angle marked, drill a ³⁄₄" hole in each back leg,

matching the angle of the arm. Then cut the back end of the arms (see photo above).

With the chair still dry fit, hold the arms in place, allowing the shoulder of the round-tenon joint to flush to the back leg of the chair. Then measure the distance from the back leg to the top of the front leg and transfer this measurement to each arm. Use this location to mark where the through-mortise is to be cut for the front leg's through-tenon.

The top of the front leg serves as a through-tenon for the arm and a ¹⁄₈"

shoulder is cut on all four sides of the leg, 1" from the top, reducing the thickness of the leg to 1¹⁄₂" at the tenon. But first, make the through-mortise in the arms. Then use the through-mortise to mark the top of the front leg. Set your table saw to cut the top of the leg to fit the mortise. Cutting the peak on the front leg is done on the table saw with the blade set at 7°.

With the chair again dry assembled, fit the arms to the front and back legs. Then mark the underside of the arms for the slat mortises. Cut this ¹⁄₄" × 3" × ¹⁄₂" deep mortise free-hand as described ear-

I used a router with a guide bushing and a template for making the through-mortise on the arm. Take it slow and make it tight, then use a file to square out the corners.

lier with the back slats. Then scribe the curve of the arm to the top edge of the side slat, (leaving $\frac{1}{2}$" for the tenon) to the underside of the arm and cut the curve on the band saw. Next, cut the tenon on the table saw to match the curve of the end. Cut out the corbels on the band saw using the template in the diagrams. Then do one more dry fit to check all the parts, and you're ready to start sanding.

Sanding & Finishing

Sand all parts to #150 grit with a random orbit sander. I chose to finish all the pieces prior to assembly to avoid runs. This gave me a very even and clean-looking finish. I first taped off all the glue joint areas, then applied a gel stain with a predominant red tint, wiping the stain to an even color. I then applied a medium-brown glaze, wiping it to an even color that I liked. I let this all dry for four hours, then sprayed on three coats of lacquer, sanding between coats.

After letting the finish cure overnight, I assembled the chair. To secure the rockers, I used a $2\frac{1}{2}$" × $\frac{3}{4}$" dowel slotted on both ends at right angles to each other. These slots are for wedges. The first wedge is put into a slot and cut so $\frac{1}{8}$" is left sticking out. When the dowel is driven into the hole with the slot and wedge going into the hole first, the wedge will be forced into the slot and will spread the dowel inside the hole in the leg, locking it into place. Another dowel is driven into

the other slot and driven home to wedge the rocker in place (see photo).

For extra holding power where the arms join the back legs, I drilled a pilot hole and put a screw into the tenon on the arm. I plugged the hole with the same wood that I used for the inlays.

Seat & Back Cushions

The seat is a 6"-thick firm foam pad with a sewn upholstery cover. The back pad measures about 2" thick and is filled with a batting material. The back cushion hangs over the back rail of the chair on straps which button to the back of the cushion to hold it in place.

A $\frac{3}{4}$" dowel with slots and wedges will hold the rockers in place for many years to come.

All-Weather Morris Chair

BY DAVID THIEL

A Morris chair is a great place to settle in and do lots of things, including reading a book and watching a good rainstorm. During at least half of the year in the Midwest these things are nice to do outside, as well as inside, but dragging a white oak mortise-and-tenoned Morris chair onto your deck isn't the easiest thing. Not one to be put out of a comfortable position, I decided painted pine could work for a Morris chair as well, and so I headed for the home improvement store.

The chair invitingly posed on my deck at left is made entirely from 1×4 and 1×6 pine, about $50 worth. The hardest joint on this chair is a butt joint, and if you've got a jigsaw, drill and a hammer you can knock one out in a day. With the help of a couple extra tools, my personal best time is just under four hours. Your hardest work will be picking through the lumber racks to find the straightest and most knot-free lumber from the store.

The chair is designed to have a cushion (also available from many home improvement stores), but you don't have

With the legs assembled, attach both lower side stretchers. Then place an upper stretcher in position and draw a line from the top of the angle on the back leg to the front leg. Cut the stretcher on the mark, then attach the upper stretchers, completing the two side frames.

to add one. If you don't use a cushion the chair may feel a little deep when you sit in it. Because of this, I'd suggest taking 2" off the lengths for the side rails, arms, seat slats and side cleats. Readjust the spacing of the side slats to fit the shorter seat.

Start your building by cutting out the pieces to form the front and rear legs.

Traditional Morris chairs typically have very stout legs, and I didn't want to lose that look or stability, so I edge-glued and nailed two pieces together to form a "T." Face-on or from the side the sturdy leg is still visible. With the legs formed, the rear (shorter) legs need to have the top end cut at a 5° angle from front to back. Remember that the back on these legs

All-Weather Morris Chair

NO.	ITEM	DIMENSIONS (INCHES)			MATERIAL	COMMENTS
		T	W	L		
2	Front legs	3/4	3 1/2	22	Pine	
2	Front legs	3/4	2 3/4	22	Pine	
2	Rear legs	3/4	3 1/2	20 1/8	Pine	Bevel to fit
2	Rear legs	3/4	2 3/4	20 1/8	Pine	Miter to fit
6	Stretchers	3/4	3 1/2	27	Pine	Miter 2 to fit
2	Arms	3/4	5 1/2	37	Pine	Trim to length
10	Side slats	3/4	3 1/2	17 1/2	Pine	Miter to fit
2	Back stiles	3/4	1 1/2	30	Pine	
2	Back stiles	3/4	2	30	Pine	
2	Back rails	3/4	3 1/2	21	Pine	
1	Back rail	3/4	1 1/2	17	Pine	
5	Back slats	3/4	1 1/2	27	Pine	
1	Back support	3/4	2	28	Pine	Bevel to fit
4	Seat cleats	3/4	1 1/2	27	Pine	Bevel 2 to fit
3	Seat slats	3/4	3 1/2	26 1/2	Pine	Trim to fit
4	Seat slats	3/4	1 1/2	26 1/2	Pine	Trim to fit
2	Dowels		1/2	2	Pine	
1	Hinge		1 1/2	20	Pine	
4	Foot rest legs	3/4	1 1/4	13 1/2	Pine	
4	foot rest legs	3/4	2	13 1/2	Pine	
2	foot rest sides	3/4	3 1/2	22 1/2	Pine	
2	foot rest sides	3/4	3 1/2	16	Pine	
4	foot rest slats	3/4	2 1/2	16	Pine	
2	cleats	3/4	3/4	17	Pine	

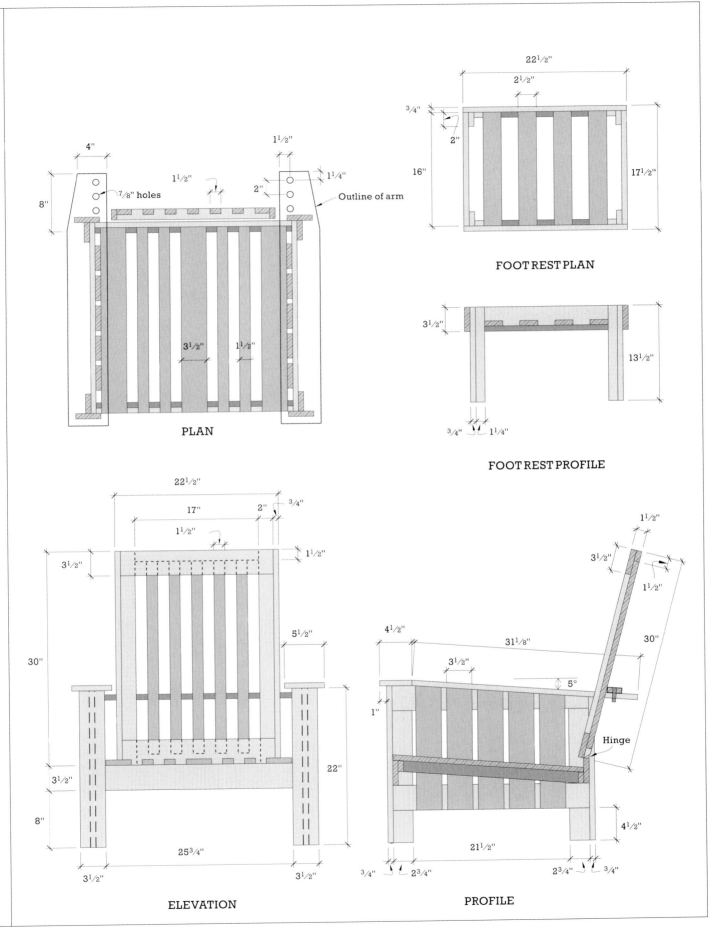

4"

1 1/2"

1 1/2"

2"

1 1/4"

8"

7/8" holes

Outline of arm

3 1/2"

1 1/2"

PLAN

22 1/2"

2 1/2"

3/4"

2"

16"

17 1/2"

FOOT REST PLAN

3 1/2"

13 1/2"

3/4"

1 1/4"

FOOT REST PROFILE

22 1/2"

17"

2"

3/4"

1 1/2"

1 1/2"

3 1/2"

5 1/2"

30"

22"

3 1/2"

8"

25 3/4"

3 1/2"

3 1/2"

ELEVATION

1 1/2"

3 1/2"

1 1/2"

30"

4 1/2"

31 1/8"

3 1/2"

5°

1"

Hinge

4 1/2"

3/4"

2 3/4"

21 1/2"

2 3/4"

3/4"

PROFILE

Simply screw the front and rear stretcher between the side frames and it starts to look like a chair.

is the top of the "T." A miter box made quick work of this step.

The next step is to get your box of 1¼" deck screws out and attach the lower side rails to the inside of the legs with the top edge 8" off the floor. With those rails attached, slip the top rails into place, flush with the front leg, and mark and cut the bevel on the rail to allow the arms of the chair to slope back. Then screw these rails in place, also on the inside of the legs. With the side frames complete, cut the pieces for the side slats using the sides themselves to determine the angle

to cut on the top of the slats. I spaced them evenly and used a pneumatic brad nailer to attach the slats as they're more decorative than structural – and it was a lot faster.

The two arms are cut from 37"-long pieces. Measure 4½" in from the front edge of each, then crosscut the pieces at this point at a 2½° angle. By flipping over the shorter piece, a 5° angle is formed, and the arms can be attached to the legs and top rails. Cut the slight bevel (shown in the diagrams) on the back of the arms to add a little more grace to the piece,

then center the arms on the front legs and nail in place.

The seat of the chair is formed by simply adding nailing cleats to the inside of the chair frame. Screw the rear cleat in place with the bottom edge flush to the bottom of the rear seat rail. Then lay a straightedge on the rear cleat, stretching across the front rail of the chair. This is the angle the seat will take. Mount the front cleat to the front rail so that it fits under the straightedge. The two side cleats are mounted following the angle of the straightedge. Mounting the seat slats is simple from here. Cut the slats and use a router to round over at least the front edges of the boards. If you like, go ahead and round over the top edges as well. Then simply lay the two outside slats tight against the sides and back and nail them in place. Put the center slat in place next, then fill in with the four thinner slats, spacing them evenly.

The back is constructed by forming L-shaped sides, screwing a top and bottom rail between them, then nail the slats evenly spaced across the back. To allow the back to fold both forward and back, the continuous hinge needs to be mounted to the inside of the back chair rail and to the outside of the lower back rail. Mounted this way the two sides will keep the back from reclining. To solve this I cut a bevel on the back rails using a hand saw. Then mount the back and fold it forward for now.

The side slats are mounted flush to the bottom of the lower side rail and cut to match the angle of the top rail. Simply hold the piece in place, make a mark, and choose your toothed tool of choice to make the cut.

The arms are cut to the front and rear lengths at a 2½° angle and then the front piece is flipped upside-down. This gives you a 5° angle at the joint. While the inner part of the arm is well supported by the legs and stretchers, the outer part of the arm needs some extra support. With a little variation on the Arts & Crafts exposed joinery theme I used a through-biscuit, cutting the biscuit slot at the mating point of the arm, then inserting the biscuit and later cutting and sanding it flush.

As you can see on the end, the back stiles are glued together to form "L"-shaped sides, then the back rails are screwed in place between the two sides. The $1\frac{1}{2}$" rail is attached to the upper rail to make a more solid looking and feeling back.

To make the chair an adjustable recliner, cut a support bar as shown in the schedule and run a chamfer along one edge. Then mark the bar as shown in the diagrams and drill two $\frac{3}{4}$" holes through the piece. Put a little glue on the two 2"-long sections of dowel and insert them into the holes until they are flush with the top edge of the piece. The glue should hold, but to add a little extra strength I tagged a brad nail through the back of the piece into each dowel.

Next mark the $\frac{7}{8}$" hole locations on the arms and drill the holes using a spade bit. To avoid tearout, drill through the top of the arm until the tip of the bit pokes through the bottom of the arm, then drill the rest of the hole coming up from the underside of the arm.

It's not a decent Morris chair unless it's got a foot rest. This one is fairly simple, with the four legs again using the strength formed by an L-shaped glue-up. Four stretchers screwed between give the footstool its shape, and cleats and some evenly spaced slats finish the job. Again, this is designed for a cushion, so if you aren't using a cushion, adjust your dimensions and mount the slats to the top of the stretchers.

You're ready to finish. Do a little sanding to knock off the sharp edges and make a nice surface on the arms. The best outdoor finish is one that blocks light and seals the wood. Around my neighborhood that's a good description of paint. I picked a nice kelly green and used about seven cans of Krylon spray paint.

You may have noticed the reference to my "best time" at the beginning of this project. Since building the first of these chairs I've built a second for myself, and there have been orders pouring in from family, friends and neighbors. So why don't some of you entrepreneurs out there take these plans and start up a summer business. Please, take some pressure off me!

With the back slats in place, the ends of the back sides need to be beveled back to allow the back to recline to a comfortable position. I'm beveling the pieces here with a pull saw at more of an angle than necessary, but it won't hurt anything.

The completed back is screwed in place against the back seat rail with a continuous hinge. You can also see the three holes in the back edge of the arms that the back support drops into.

Gustav Stickley's Morris Chair

BY ROBERT W. LANG

In Gustav Stickley's book *Craftsman Homes*, there is a picture of this chair with the following caption: "A big deep chair that means comfort to a tired man when he comes home after the day's work." First produced around 1906, this chair is an icon of Stickley's furniture and his philosophy. Visually, this chair invites you to sit down and relax – a result of the sloping arms and side rails, the warmth and color of the quartersawn white oak and the upholstered seat and back. Few people can resist the desire to sit in it. And few who sit in it can rise without regret.

Other manufacturers who knocked off Stickley's work cut corners and simplified his designs, and many woodworkers look for a way to make a chair like this with simpler joinery. Without the joinery it isn't a chair like this; it's something less. There is a reward for doing it right; in this case, the reward for the effort is the chair itself.

Fools Rush In

As I prepare to build, I like to break a project down into its component parts. Each side of the base of this chair is a subassembly of two legs connected with rails. These are joined with rails front and back and are capped with the distinctive bent arms. The back of the chair is a separate unit that pivots and adjusts with a simple mechanism.

One obvious challenge is making the arm, but that is simpler than it seems. The rails and slats below the arms seem simple, but the slope that makes the chair appealing complicates these parts.

The first step in making this chair is to draw a full-size layout of the side assembly. It's a good exercise in understanding how it all goes together, and it's a crucial reference for the actual sizes and angles of the component parts.

The top edge of the top side rail is angled, rising from a height of $^{15}/_{16}$" at the back leg to the full width of $3^1/_2$" at a point $3/_4$" behind the front leg. The bottom edge of this rail is parallel to the floor, and perpendicular to the legs. The bottom rail is a constant width, but it meets the legs at a slight angle; the back is $3/_4$" lower than the front.

That slope makes the through-tenons on each end of the lower rail a little

A full-scale drawing provides a reference for most parts of the project. It saves time, and prevents measurement and layout errors.

trickier, but the real complication is that each of the vertical slats is a different length. After drawing the full-size view, I switched gears and made the legs, which gave me something useful to do as I pondered the implications of the angled ends of the slats.

Trees Don't Grow Like That

Quartersawn figure on all four sides of the legs was a feature of original versions of this chair, and I used the same method used in Stickley's Craftsman Workshops. Three pieces of $^{13}/_{16}$"-thick material were laminated into a stack. After letting the glue cure overnight, I dressed the surfaces on the jointer.

Then I glued a $^1/_8$"-thick piece of quartersawn wood to the side edges of the leg laminations. These thick veneers were sliced on the band saw and cover the unattractive side grain (as well as the joint lines) on the legs. After an overnight wait for the glue to cure, the legs were dressed down to $2^3/_8$" square.

The edges of the legs are beveled, with the bevel ending at the glue line between the solid and veneered edges. I placed the finished legs on the full-size layout to locate the tenons at the tops, and the mortises, marking the locations directly on the legs from the drawing.

I made the $^5/_8$"-wide through-mortises with a hollow-chisel mortiser, working from both sides with a $^1/_2$" chisel and bit. That size bit takes less effort to plunge into the work, and I centered the mortises by cutting one side of the joint, then flipped the workpiece so the opposite side was against the machine's fence.

I also cut the angle on the back legs, and the $1^1/_2$" square tenons on the tops of all the legs before proceeding. The tenons on the ends of the side rails were cut, and I dry-fit test assemblies of the sides. I

located the taper for the top rail from the test assembly and after cutting it on the band saw, I put each side assembly on top of my drawing.

Use This to Measure That

I marked the locations of the vertical slats on the top and bottom rails, along with the mortises for the slats. Then, with a lumber crayon I marked each mortise with a number. I put each slat in position, numbered each with the crayon and marked the shoulder locations directly from the rails.

Each vertical slat is a bit longer than its neighbor, and if the slats move sideways along the rail the length will change. A slat that is slightly long or short can be moved for appearance sake, but more than a slight adjustment will show as inconsistent gaps between the slats. Moving one slat laterally will also affect the fit of an adjacent slat.

Many Mortises

The mortises in the rails are centered and I made them with a $^3/_8$"-wide chisel in the mortising machine. I saved the offcuts from the top rails and temporarily reattached them with tape to keep the mortises vertical. I cut a long wedge to

Tapered scrap

A tapered piece of scrap below the workpiece keeps the mortises oriented vertically.

The offcuts from tapering the upper rails are taped back in place to keep the clamps from sliding during assembly.

Because the lower end of the vertical slats are angled, they only fit in one place. They can be adjusted with a tap or two.

Start the through-tenon in the mortise before brushing on the glue to keep the end of the tenon clean.

With the sides glued into units, the last stage of the base assembly is a simple matter.

hold the bottom rail at the correct angle to keep those mortises vertical.

I cut all of the tenon shoulders by hand. That gave me more control over the angles and a better cut edge than cutting them by machine. I cut the tenon cheeks on the band saw, and adjusted the fit with a shoulder plane and a float. When the slats were fit to the two rails I made a trial run of that subassembly with the legs.

I made a few minor adjustments to get a good fit everywhere. Before gluing the slats in position, I smoothed all the edges of the rails and slats with my plane and rounded all the edges slightly.

Gustav Stickley's Morris Chair

NO.	ITEM	DIMENSIONS (INCHES)			MATERIAL	COMMENTS
		T	W	L		
2	Front legs	$2^3/_8$	$2^3/_8$	$23^1/_2$	QSWO	$1^1/_4$ TOE
2	Back legs	$2^3/_8$	$2^3/_8$	$20^7/_8$	QSWO	$1^1/_4$ TOE
12	Leg laminations	$13/_{16}$	$2^3/_8$	25	QSWO	
8	Leg veneers	$1/_8$	3	25	QSWO	
2	Top side rail	$7/_8$	$3^1/_2$	$24^5/_8$	QSWO	TBE
2	Bottom side rails	$7/_8$	3	$27^3/_8$	QSWO	TBE
10	Side slats	$5/_8$	$2^7/_8$	16	QSWO	TBE
1	Low front rail	$7/_8$	$4^3/_8$	$28^1/_4$	QSWO	TBE
1	Low back rail	$7/_8$	$3^3/_4$	$28^1/_4$	QSWO	TBE
2	Arms	$15/_{16}$	$5^3/_8$	$35^3/_4$	QSWO	
4	Corbels	$1^1/_8$	2	$9^7/_8$	QSWO	
2	Doughnuts	$5/_{16}$	2 dia.		QSWO	
2	Pivot pins	1	1	$5^3/_4$	QSWO	
2	Stop pins	1	1	$3^3/_4$	QSWO	
2	Back stiles	$1^1/_2$	$1^3/_4$	$26^{11}/_{16}$	QSWO	
1	Top back slat	$3/_4$	$3^1/_2$	$21^3/_8$	QSWO	TBE bent lamination
4	Back slats	$3/_4$	$2^3/_4$	$21^3/_8$	QSWO	TBE bent lamination
2	Seat cleats	$3/_4$	1	$22^7/_8$	QSWO	

QSWO = quartersawn white oak; TOE = tenon, one end; TBE = tenon, both ends

Through & Through

The through-tenons on the bottom rails give the chair frame strength – if they fit well. They also need to look good from the outside. Good looks are a given if the joints fit, and the key to it all is planning and patience.

The mortise walls need to be straight and consistent, so I spent some time with a float to even out rough areas left from the hollow chisel. I also made sure that the ends were square and the walls of the mortises were perpendicular to the faces of the legs. With a chisel, I cut a small bevel on the inside edge of each mortise to ease starting the tenons.

To determine the exact tenon width,

I held the end of a rail against the long edge of a mortise, and made a pencil mark to transfer the width of the mortise. I then took my marking gauge and set it halfway between the pencil mark and the opposite face of the rail. I made a test mark from each side and held the end of the rail to the mortise to check that the widths matched.

When I was satisfied that I had the correct size for the tenons, I marked the edges and ends of the rails with my gauge. I clamped both rails together and marked the shoulder locations at the same time to be sure they matched. The shoulder cuts are only 1/8" deep, and I cut these by hand at a bench hook using my backsaw.

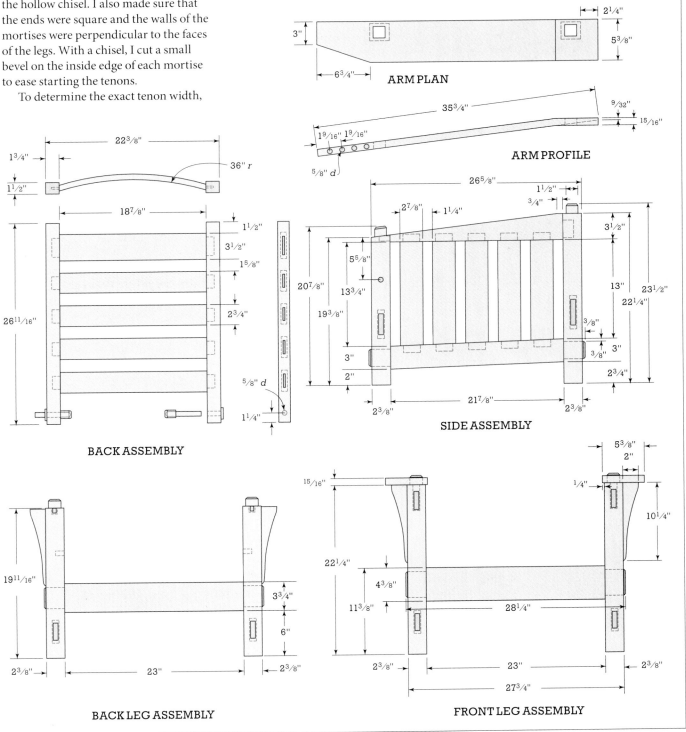

ARM PLAN

ARM PROFILE

BACK ASSEMBLY

SIDE ASSEMBLY

BACK LEG ASSEMBLY

FRONT LEG ASSEMBLY

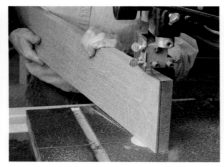

An angled wedge sliced off the end of the arm forms the bend.

The wedge is glued to the underside of the arm, smooth face to smooth face.

Planing out the band saw marks leaves a smooth surface on the top and bottom of the arm.

The glue line should disappear because the grain and color are the same in both pieces.

Balance the arm on the base assembly and mark the location of both the front and back tenons without moving the arm.

An adjustable bevel transfers the layout lines for the angled mortise from the top of the arm to the bottom.

At the band saw, I set the fence so that a tooth angled toward the fence was just outside the marked line. I held the rails against the fence and cut the wide cheeks back to almost the shoulder line. I measured the tenon and the mortise with dial calipers to compare the sizes. My goal was a fence setting that left the tenon barely thicker than the mortise. This prevents a sloppy tenon, but it means that some tweaking must be done to get a good fit.

Before fitting, I cut a chamfer on the end of each tenon. This makes it easy to insert the tenon for a test fit, and it keeps the end of the tenon from doing any damage to the outer edges of the mortise when it comes through.

Fitting involves removing a small amount of material at a time and seeing how far the tenon will go into the mortise. I generally start with a shoulder plane, taking care not to introduce

a taper in the tenon. As I get closer, I switch to a float, which is easier to control and leaves a nicer surface.

Hatch marks made with a pencil on the tenon indicate high spots that keep the joint from going home. The graphite smears at the sticking points, and I used the float to take off the smeared spots. I don't use a mallet to drive the tenon in; too much force can cause a break.

Hand pressure is enough, and when the tenon can be inserted about two-thirds of the way, I can look from the outside to see if there are any problem areas. The first assembly is the hardest. I usually take joints apart and put them back together several times as I'm working to tune the fit at the shoulder and to make trial runs before making a final assembly with glue and clamps.

When I was happy with the fit, I marked with a pencil where the outside of the leg lands on the exposed tenon. I cut the tenon 1/4" beyond that line, then chamfered the end of the tenon back to the line with a block plane, rasp and finally sandpaper. Leaving the line ensures that the visible intersection of the tenon and the leg looks tight.

Bring on the Glue

Assembly of the base of the chair is done in stages; first the vertical slats are glued between the top and bottom rails for each side. I used liquid hide glue to gain some extra open time, and held the angled offcut from the top rail in place with painter's tape to keep the clamps from sliding. I used a block of soft wood and a mallet to fine-tune the lateral position of the slats.

I let that dry in the clamps overnight, and glued the legs to each end of the rail assemblies the following morning. To keep glue from going everywhere around the through-mortises, I started the tenons in the holes, then brushed glue on the cheeks before assembling and clamping the joints.

After letting the rail-to-leg joints dry overnight, I marked and drilled a 5/8"-diameter hole 1 3/8" deep on the inside of each of the back legs. I then connected the two side assemblies with the front and back rails. This assembly was also left in the clamps overnight.

The arms complete the side assemblies, and are cut from a piece of 15/16" × 5 3/8" stock. I started with a piece several inches longer than the finished length to get the angle of the bend and the tenon locations right first. Before making the arm, I made sure that the top edges of the top rails were in line with the shoulders on the tops of the legs.

I placed the stock of an adjustable bevel on the shoulder of the front leg, and set the blade to the slope of the rail. I transferred this angle to the edge of the arm. The bend is actually a tapered slice cut from the top of the leg, then glued to the bottom edge.

After making the cut on the band saw, I glued the wedge to the bottom of the arm. This leaves the sawn edges exposed on the top and bottom surfaces of the arm, and the previously surfaced faces glued together. I removed the saw marks with my plane.

Location, Location, Location

The through-mortises on the arms are the most visible joints in the chair, and there aren't any magic tricks or shortcuts to the process. The mortises need to be just right, and in just the right place. I flipped the assembled base of the chair on its side so I could locate the joints in each arm directly from the tenons.

I placed the arm on top of the tenons in the legs, lining up the angle in the arm with the angle in the top rail behind the front leg. With a square I carried the edges of the tenon around both the top and bottom face of the arm. The procedure was roughly the same for the back tenon, except that I used an adjustable bevel to carry the lines over the edges.

When the chair is finished, the arm extends $1/4$" past the leg on the inside. I measured from the side of the leg to the cheek of the tenon, added the $1/4$" and marked the side of the mortise on the upper and lower faces of the arm. I then measured the tenon width and marked that distance on the face of the arm for the second edge of the mortise.

An accurate layout is half the battle so I stepped back and double-checked my lines before cutting. I removed most of the waste inside the lines with a $3/4$" Forstner bit at the drill press. For the front mortises, I placed a block of wood below the arm to support the horizontal end level while drilling.

At the back of the arm, I cut a wedge

from a scrap of 8/4 material to support the arm while drilling to keep the front and back edges of the mortises plumb. I used this same wedge to support the arm on the bench as I pared the mortise walls back to the layout lines.

I worked carefully and checked frequently to avoid over-cutting the mortises. It isn't possible to check the fit of the tenons one at a time. As with the through-tenons connecting the rails and legs, I beveled the ends of the tenons and hidden edges of the mortises before fitting, and used pencil marks on the tenons to locate any high spots.

When I had a good fit, I marked the top edge of the arms on the leg tenons, then removed the arms and rounded over the exposed ends of the tenons with a block plane and rasp. Before permanently attaching the arms, I drilled a series of $5/8$"-diameter holes on the inside back edges for the support pins.

Back in a Week

While waiting for the glue to dry on the base assemblies, I made the curved

Supplies

Tools for Working Wood
toolsforworkingwood.com or
800-426-4613

W.D. Lockwood's Fumed Oak (#94) alcohol-soluble aniline dye, 1 oz., $7.49

Price as of publication date.

back slats. I built a form from four layers of $3/4$"-thick particle board cut to a 36" radius. I cut the curve on the first layer at the band saw, then smoothed the edge. The remaining edges were cut oversize, and each layer was added to the stack, then trimmed to the previous layer with a flush-cutting router bit.

Each slat consists of six $1/8$"-thick layers. I marked a triangle on the edge of the slat blanks to keep the pieces in order, and made the cuts on the band saw. With a decent saw cut, the laminations can be glued without any further smoothing. I used a 3" paint roller to apply yellow glue, put the stacked pieces against the form and started clamping from the middle

A wedge below the arm provides the proper tilt to keep the holes vertical.

The same wedge is clamped between the arm and the bench to pare down the walls of the through-mortise.

Check the size frequently with calipers as you work on the mortise, and compare it to the tenon.

Mark the intersection of the arm and the tenon with a pencil line and round the end of the tenon down to the edge. Stop just outside the line to maintain the fit between the two parts.

Work fast. Use a roller to spread glue on one side only of the laminations for the back. Keep the pieces in order and the edges will match.

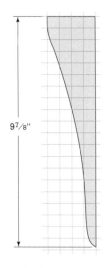

CORBEL PATTERN
Each square = ¹⁄₂"

9⁷⁄₈"

What the Holes Are For

Wooden pins serve as pivots for the back, and as stops to adjust the back to any of four positions. I started with four 1"-square blocks about 8" long and turned a ⁵⁄₈"-diameter shaft on one half. These could also be made by gluing a dowel into a hole drilled in the end of a square block. I sanded the shafts to reduce the diameter slightly. These should go easily in and out of the holes in the arms and back legs.

After fitting the pins, I trimmed them to length. The bottom pins pass through the stiles of the back, and the round shafts are about 2" longer than the depth of the holes in the back legs. The upper set of pins are the same depth as the holes, and the square section should be about 2" long.

I used a block plane to chamfer the edges of the square end of the pins to an octagon shape and to round off the ends. Round wooden washers hold the back assembly away from the legs. These are 2" in diameter, and I waited until the arms were glued to the base, and the back was assembled, to make them.

I used a piece of scrap 2" wide and 12" long, and aimed for a thickness half the difference between the back and the back legs. Then I took another ¹⁄₃₂" off the thickness before drilling the holes and cutting the outside to a circular shape. These doughnuts keep the back from rubbing on the arms, but they must be thin enough to allow the back to swing without binding.

The last pieces to be fabricated are the

out to each end.

I used a piece of ¹⁄₄"-thick Plexiglas between the wood and the clamps to spread the pressure and prevent clamp marks on the wood, and left each stack on the form overnight. When all five slats were finished, I scraped the excess glue from the edges, ran one edge over the jointer, then trimmed the slats to width on the table saw.

To lay out the tenons on the ends of the curved pieces, I prepared a straight stick with a tenon on each end. By placing this stick on the top edge of the slats, I was able to mark the tenons on the curved parts by tracing. I then carried the lines around the slats with a square and an adjustable bevel.

I made the shoulder cuts by hand after

going over the layout lines with a knife. The slats stayed put on the bench hook with the convex side of the curve on top. To cut the other side, with the curve up, I put a wedge of scrap below the slat and held the slats to the bench with a clamp while I made the cuts. I cut the cheeks at the band saw.

The ¹⁄₄"-wide, 1"-deep mortises in the back stiles are centered in the thickness of the rails, and were cut with the hollow-chisel mortiser. Before assembly, I sanded all the parts for the back, chamfered the edges of the stiles and drilled the holes at the bottom of the stiles.

When assembled, the width of the back should be about ¹⁄₈" less than the distance between the arms to allow the back to adjust without interference.

Make a pattern on scrap to lay out the tenon locations on the curved back rails. Hold the stick in place and mark both ends without moving the stick.

Mark the tenons all the way around the slat with a square and an adjustable bevel. Go over the lines with a knife before cutting the shoulders with a backsaw.

A band saw is an efficient way to cut the tenon cheeks, or you can cut them by hand. Either way, cut a little wide and make the tenons fit with a shoulder plane or a float.

four corbels that support the outer halves of the arms at each leg. All four corbels are cut to the pattern from $1^1/8$"-thick stock. The back corbels should be about $1/2$" shorter in the straight section than the front. The top of the back corbels also must be angled to match the slope at the top of the back legs below the arms.

The corbels are centered on the legs and are held to the leg with glue and a screw in a plugged hole. The screw isn't necessary as the glue alone would be strong enough, but it makes it easier to hold the corbel in position. Without the screw, the corbels slide around as the clamps are tightened.

When the glue holding the corbels dried, the screw holes were filled with dowels. The through-tenons on the base assembly were also pinned with dowels, as well as the tenons in the top and bottom slats of the back assembly.

I make dowels from straight-grained scrap. I start with a piece about 3" long and split blanks from the scrap with a chisel or a stout knife. I then drive the dowels through holes in a $1/4$"-thick steel dowel plate. I whittle the ends to get them started, and knock off the corners with a chisel so there is less material to remove.

The dowels are coated with glue and driven into place. Once dry, the pegs are trimmed flush with a saw. The saw can leave a fraction of the plug proud of the surface, so a bit of paring with a chisel was needed in a couple places.

Hard Surfaces, Soft Surfaces
As I worked, I smoothed exposed faces and edges with my planes before assembling. I also chamfered the long edges with my block plane, and I used a rasp and sandpaper to round the exposed tenons. In a few places I had some tear-out to deal with where the grain direction reversed, and I used a card scraper to smooth these troublemakers.

Each of these tools leaves a smooth surface, but with a slightly different texture. To get an even texture before finishing, I sanded the entire chair, first with #120-grit Abranet, then #180 grit. Sanding white oak to too fine a grit can polish the surface to a point where it won't absorb color evenly. If scratches from sanding aren't visible, the wood is smooth enough to dye.

After turning one end of the pin, trim it to length then shave the sides to an octagon. The last step is to round the end to a hand-friendly dome shape.

The back of the chair pivots on the lower set of pins, and the large wooden washers keep the back centered without rubbing on the arms. The upper pins support the back in one of four positions, from upright to do not disturb.

Dowels cover screws that hold the corbels to the legs. The through-mortises on the legs are also pegged with dowels made from scraps. Trim them flush before finishing.

I used W.D. Lockwood's Fumed Oak (#94) aniline dye dissolved in alcohol. This dries quickly as it is brushed on and doesn't raise the grain. I aimed for a consistent coat on all surfaces without running the dye. The color is close to that of white oak fumed with ammonia, and there is another similarity between the dye and fuming; the surface looks like you ruined it when it dries.

I rubbed the entire chair with an abrasive pad after letting the dye dry for a few hours, then brushed on a 50-50 mixture of clear and amber shellac. I diluted this about a third with alcohol. The following morning I went over the chair again with the abrasive pad, then brushed on a second coat of shellac. After letting the shellac cure for a week, I gave the chair a coat of Dark Watco Satin wax, applied with an abrasive pad then buffed with a cotton cloth.

I had a local upholstery shop make the cushions. The bottom cushion rests on $3/4$" × 1" cleats screwed to the inside of the front and back rails, $1^1/4$" down from the top edge. The cushion consists of a solid-wood frame made of 2×4 material, ripped to 2" wide.

The corners are mitered and held together with glue and screws, with 45° corner blocks for additional strength. Rubber webbing was stapled to the top edge of the frame. The webbing covers the entire opening, running in both directions in a basketweave.

A 1"-thick, 12"-square piece of high density foam was glued to the center of the webbing to give the cushion a crown. On top of this is a 4"-thick piece of high-density foam wrapped in Dacron. The fabric wraps over the foam and is stapled to the bottom of the wood frame.

The back cushion is a 2"-thick piece of soft foam wrapped twice in Dacron. The buttons in the back of this cushion help it to conform to the curve of the back, and loops of fabric hold the cushion in place on the back frame.

The Roorkhee Chair

BY CHRISTOPHER SCHWARZ

Furniture historians tend to paint the Arts & Crafts movement as a turning point for modern furniture design – where style turned its back on the ornate excesses of the Victorians to embrace the simple lines of what was to become the more utilitarian furniture of the 20th century.

I won't dispute that assessment, but it neglects a long-overlooked piece of furniture: the Roorkhee chair. Named after the British headquarters of the Indian Army Corps of Engineers in India, the Roorkhee chair was developed in the final years of the 19th century as the British military became more mobile following humiliations it suffered in South Africa during the Boer Wars (1880–81 and 1899–1902).

Weighing under 13 pounds, the Roorkhee chair breaks down quickly, takes up little space and is shockingly comfy. Because it has no fixed joinery, the legs and stretchers move to accommodate uneven terrain and any sitter.

It was a mainstay of the British army and navy up until World War II, according to Nicholas A. Brawer's book *British Campaign Furniture* (Abrams). And it also appears as a popular item for campers, adventurers and those on safari.

While all that is quite interesting, what is more fascinating is how the work-a-day Roorkhee chair directly influenced generations of modern furniture designers. Marcel Breuer's "Wassily" chair (1925) and Wilhelm Bofinger's "Farmer Chair" (1966), among others, owe a tremendous debt to the Roorkhee chair.

One summer I built a run of these chairs for customers and for a book I wrote about campaign-style furniture, and I selected one of the simpler forms of the Roorkhee to reproduce. To build it you need only 10 sticks of wood, a handful of tools and some upholstery. You can easily get the upholstery made in canvas by anyone with a sewing machine, or you can take the route I did and use cowhide, which is surprisingly simple work. Either material is historically correct.

Begin with the Legs

The 1¾"-square legs are beefier than modern examples of Roorkhee chairs, so resist the urge to skimp on material. The historical examples I've examined are made using mahogany or oak, so you

can take the high road or the low one, depending on your budget.

Begin by shaping the legs. The cylinder at the top of each leg and the ankle at the floor are both 1¼" in diameter. So if you aren't confident in your lathe skills, you can waste away some of the material by using a dado stack in your table saw before chucking the work up between centers in your lathe.

Turn the round sections of the leg down to shape using a roughing gouge. Get the cylinder and ankle to size using a parting tool and skew. Use a skew to finish up the taper on the legs and the transitions, and a spindle gouge to create the ¾"-tall astragal that makes the foot. (Just FYI, I turned these legs with the full-size Easy Rougher [$129.99, easywoodtools.com], which will do all the operations on these legs with ease.)

Once you have the legs turned, make the ⅞"-radius curve on the top of each leg. Cut it to rough shape with a coping saw, then finish the job with a rasp or disc sander.

Tapered Joinery

Like a Windsor chair, Roorkhee chairs are assembled using tapered tenons and conical mortises. Unlike Windsor chairs, however, these joints are left loose – no glue and no wedges. Still, you want a good fit.

A Roorkhee chair has four 1"-diameter round rails, which you can make simply by using dowel stock (or turn them on your lathe). Original chairs would offer a seat that was about 16½" wide and deep between the legs, which is skimpy for modern backsides. The sizes shown in this article will create a chair that has a seat that's 18" square between the legs. If you need more room, use longer dowels. But don't go overboard – longer dowels weaken the chair.

Begin by drilling a ½"-diameter hole for the dowels through your legs in the locations shown in the illustrations. All these holes are 90°; if you've ever built chairs, this should be a relief.

Now ream the holes into a cone. I used the Veritas Pro Reamer, which I chucked into a brace. You can also grind a cheap spade bit to the shape you desire, which will scrape the sides of the mortise to the correct taper.

Turn the cylinder at the top of the leg with care. If your tool catches the square section above or below, game over.

The transition between the cylinder and the square section is a snap if you ease into the cut slowly.

To make the astragal at the foot, turn 45° chamfers on the corners. Then turn chamfers on the arrises of the chamfers. Then turn arrises on those chamfers until you get an astragal.

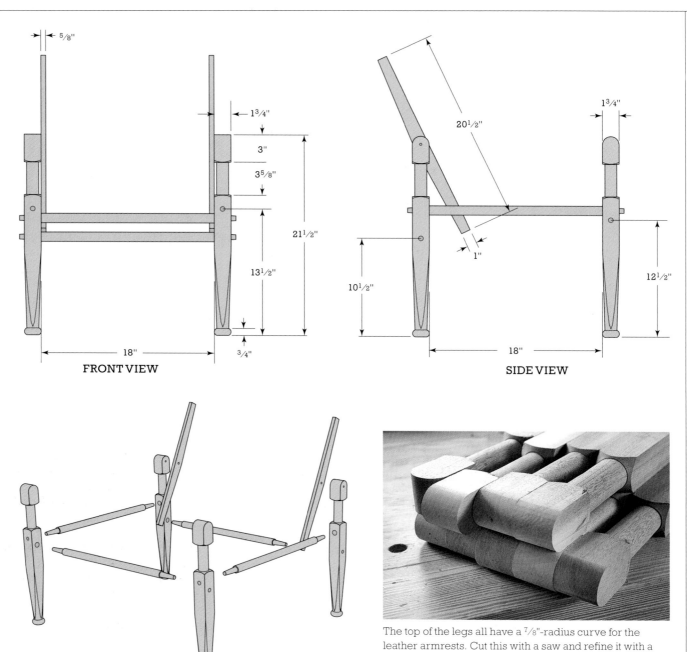

FRONT VIEW

5/8"

1 3/4"

3"

3 5/8"

21 1/2"

13 1/2"

18"

3/4"

SIDE VIEW

20 1/2"

1 3/4"

1"

10 1/2"

12 1/2"

18"

EXPLODED VIEW

The top of the legs all have a 7/8"-radius curve for the leather armrests. Cut this with a saw and refine it with a rasp or sandpaper. If you are making a run of chairs, a disc sander is a huge help.

Roorkhee Chair

NO.	ITEM	DIMENSIONS (INCHES)			MATERIAL	COMMENTS
		T	W	L		
Wood						
4	Legs	1 3/4	1 3/4	21 1/2	Mahogany	
4	Rails	1 dia.		23 1/4	Mahogany	Over-long, trim to fit
2	Back braces	5/8	1 1/2	20 1/2	Mahogany	
Leather						
2	Leg straps	3 oz.	1/2	21 3/4	Leather	Overall joined length
1	Seat support	3 oz.	4 1/2	35	Leather	
1	Seat	3 oz.	17	33	Leather	
1	Back	3 oz.	20	27	Leather	3 1/2" w. × 4 1/4" notch

A tapered reamer is the best practical solution to making the conical mortises. A sharp reamer is a joy. (A ground spade bit will also work.)

The Lee Valley Tools Tapered Tenon Cutter works like a high-quality pencil sharpener. It produces clean and crisp work.

After every reaming operation, confirm that your rails are 90° to the leg in both axes. Use your reamer to adjust the attitude of each leg.

With the mortises reamed, shape the tenons. Cut the dowels to finished length and then turn the ends to a cone shape on your lathe. Alternately, if you used the Veritas Pro Taper Reamer, you can buy the $1/2$" Tapered Tenon Cutter ($37.50, leevalley.com) and shave the dowels as if you were using a pencil sharpener.

The Back Braces
The back of a Roorkhee chair tilts to fit the user. The tilting occurs on $5/16$"-diameter all-thread steel rods that pass through the back legs and the two back braces. The braces are secured to the legs using nuts, washers and wing nuts – all available at your local hardware store.

First drill holes through the legs to accept the $5/16$" rod. The holes should be at the center of the $7/8$" radius that defines the top curve of the legs. The holes should be just a smidge larger than $5/16$" – whatever you have in your shop.

Now make the back braces. These two pieces taper from $1^1/2$" wide at the center to 1" wide at the ends. Mark the taper on the braces and taper them with a handplane (or make the cut with a band saw). To complete the braces, drill a clearance hole for the steel rod through the braces in the center of the widest part of each brace.

Finish the Wood
Remove all the tool marks from the parts, break the edges and finish all the wooden parts using three coats of garnet shellac. The wood is only one-half of this project. And you can choose to hand off the upholstery to a professional or do it yourself. (You can do it. It's easy.)

Leather & Hardware
The leather upholstery is stuff that is about 3–4 oz. cowhide – one typical skin should be more than enough for one chair. Begin by making the straps for the legs. These straps restrain the sides of the chair. Unbuckling them disassembles the chair. You can cut the straps using a straightedge and a sharp utility knife. Repeat: sharp utility knife.

Punch the holes for the buckles using an $1/8$"-diameter drive punch, available at all leather-supply stores. To attach the straps to the buckle you'll need to rivet the leather into a loop. Riveting is simplicity itself. Punch two holes in the leather. Fold the leather over so the holes meet up – wet the leather if you want to make it more bendable.

Put the male end of the rivet through the hole and place it on a hard surface (such as your table saw). Place the rivet's cap on top. Strike the rivet three times or so using a hammer and a rivet-setter – a

steel rod with a concave end. This makes a permanent join.

Screw the straps to the inside surfaces of the legs. Use #10 × $1^1/2$" brass screws and brass finishing washers – two screws in each leg. Remember that the leather will stretch in use, so install it on the tight side.

The Seat Support, Seat & Back
Your bottom and your back are supported by three pieces of leather in the Roorkhee. The back is stretched and riveted around the back braces. The seat is two pieces of leather. There's a narrow seat strap that runs from side to side, plus the main seat that runs from front to back and sits on top of the seat strap.

These three pieces are all installed in the same way. Stretch the leather over the wood and mark where the line of rivets should go. This is mostly by eye, but space the rivets about 1" apart from one another. Punch all the holes for the rivets using your $1/8$" drive punch.

Before you rivet the leather, it's best to finish it. You can burnish the edges and simply add a wax/oil solution, which is available at leatherworking stores. Or you can color the leather with a dye, finish it with an oil/leather solution and then rivet the flaps together. After you finish these leather pieces, thread everything

Riveted Leather – Not Canvas

Roorkhee chairs were covered in canvas, leather or leather-trimmed canvas. Of the three options, plain old leather is the simplest of the three solutions. However, if you prefer canvas but don't have sewing skills in your household, I recommend you outsource the job.

I think you'll be surprised how economical leather can be. I bought the skin, rivets, buckles and tools I needed for this chair for about $150.

I chose to rivet the leather pieces together for this chair. The other option is to sew them together. I decided against the sewing. Here's why.

To sew the leather together I'd either need a sewing machine that can pierce 3 oz. leather (I don't have one) or punch all the holes for the thread. I didn't want to buy or borrow a sewing machine so I decided on riveting, another traditional leatherworking joint. It requires only a punch, rivets and a rivet setter. Once you try riveting you'll be amazed how easy it is. In fact, punching and riveting leather is so easy that you might start making your own belts, suspenders or tool rolls. I'm making some chisel holders with my scraps (just be sure your leather is vegetable-tanned if you do this).

Make your templates for your leather using 1/2"-thick material – I used some MDF left over from another job.

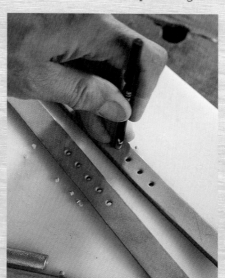

The 1/8"-diameter drive punch will do all the leather work on this chair. Keep it sharp and lubricated with beeswax or paraffin.

Simple small rivets join all the leather in this project. A steel rivet-setter and mallet does all the leather joinery.

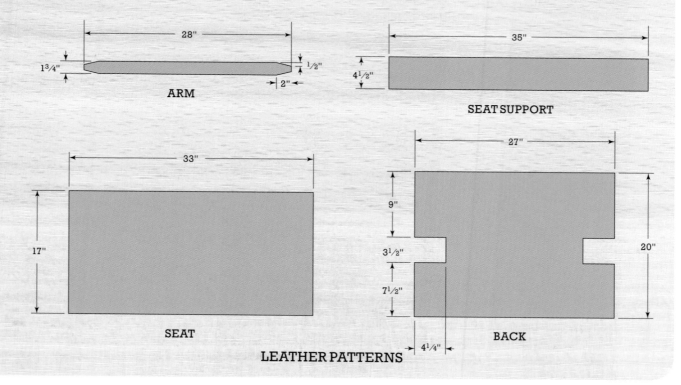

ARM
28"
1 3/4"
1/2"
2"

SEAT SUPPORT
35"
4 1/2"

SEAT
33"
17"

BACK
27"
9"
3 1/2"
7 1/2"
20"
4 1/4"

LEATHER PATTERNS

together and pull the chair together. It should hold together and sit well. The only things left to add are the armrests.

Armrests

The armrests were the biggest challenge to construct because the hardware to attach them to the chair isn't standard stuff. You can use 13mm ball socket studs, which are used to attach gas struts to car bodies – these are the struts that hold up the glass on the back of a pickup truck's camper top.

Or you can take the hard road and make your own. I used "Sam Browne" buttons from Tandy Leather. These are the stud shape you need, but instead of having a screw that goes into the wood, there's a threaded hole in the stud. I found a metric machine-screw fastener that screwed into this hole in the stud. This created a fastener that I could insert into the leg in a $\frac{7}{64}$"-diameter hole.

Whew. Or just go to an auto parts store and get the 13mm ball socket stud. It's simpler. Screw these studs into the legs.

To attach the leather to the studs, make a slot at each end of each leather armrest. Use your $\frac{1}{8}$" drive punch to define the extents of the slot, then use your utility knife to join the holes. This should make a hole that will button over the studs. Remember: Make the leather tighter than you think you

Here you can see the back braces bolted to the rear legs. The acorn nuts were later replaced with wing nuts.

should. It will loosen up.

OK, sit in the chair. Lean back and feel how it supports your lower back. Awesome, no? What? Don't fall asleep. I'm not done yet. There are still other leg profiles of Roorkhee chairs to discuss.

Oh, never mind. Enjoy your nap. Tomorrow you might have to fight.

Supplies

Tandy Leather
tandyleatherfactory.com
or 877-532-8437

- 1 • Craftsman oak tooling leather side #9157-35, $5 sq. ft. (need about 22 sq. ft.)

- 1 • Rapid rivets #1271-15, $5.99/100 ct.

- 2 • Halter buckles, $\frac{3}{4}$" #1505-00, $4.49 ea.

- 1 • $\frac{1}{8}$" drive punch #3777-02, $9.99

- 1 • Rivet setter #8100-00, $3.99

- 1 • Aussie leather conditioner #2199-00, $14.99

- 4 • Button studs #11310-01, $3.49 ea.

Prices as of publication date.

Here's the Roorkhee with brown leather, the steel 13mm ball studs and no straps on the legs. This arrangement is also historically correct.

Cheating at Chairmaking

BY CHRISTOPHER SCHWARZ ET AL.

The sticks are kiln-dried ash; the leg blanks are kiln-dried oak. By sawing them out by following the grain lines of the wood, I was able to get reasonably sturdy and workable stuff.

After building my first stick Windsor chair using traditional tools and green wood, it was like I was on crack. Like thousands of woodworkers I returned home from my first chairmaking class aching to replace every uncomfortable (and ugly) chair in our house.

But there was a problem. Several problems, actually. None of the tools in my workshop were the chairmaking tools I'd learned to use in the class. And a couple hours with a calculator and the Highland Woodworking catalog convinced me that my credit card didn't need that kind of one-time workout.

Plus there were other barriers besides tools. Getting green wood is a challenge in some cities. And making room in a crowded shop for chairmaking activities can be a head-scratcher.

I knew it was time to cheat.

So I talked to professional chairmakers and would-be bodgers about how they work around their limitations. And I focused the jig-making part of my brain on the chairmaker's universe.

And most importantly, I launched into making another set of chairs, despite the murky water ahead of me. The following pages contain the best tricks, cheats and workarounds I encountered in my search. Not all of them will work for you, your temperament or your pocketbook (though most of them are dirt-cheap solutions).

But these cheats do work for me and other chairmakers. It is our hope that some of them might help you launch your next chairmaking project.

Cheating Nature: Kiln-Dried Lumber Can Work

Building a chair with green wood that is split from a stump is a joy. The wood is easy to work and the grain is arrow-straight.

But for some of us, green wood is hard to come by. So I tried using dowel stock and spokeshaving it to size, but that was frustrating. Dowels don't have the straight grain of riven materials, which are split out along the grain using a froe.

Dowels also aren't as strong and they are difficult to spokeshave without tearout. In the end, I used a card scraper to finish up the sticks. In other words, it

was more work and didn't look as good.

John Brown, a Welsh stick chairmaker and personal hero, has used sawn stock for his sticks in the past, according to his columns published in the British magazine *Good Woodworking*. He would band saw the lumber along the grain lines and then shape it with "rounding planes,"

which are small metal and wooden gizmos that make dowels (more on those tools later).

That was good enough for me. I purchased quartersawn ash, and I sawed out my sticks by following the grain lines. My results were good. The sticks are strong and you can spokeshave them

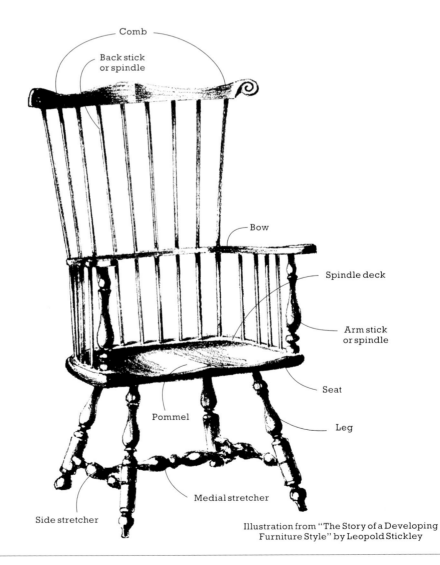

Comb

Back stick or spindle

Bow

Spindle deck

Arm stick or spindle

Seat

Pommel

Leg

Medial stretcher

Side stretcher

Illustration from "The Story of a Developing Furniture Style" by Leopold Stickley readily. It's not as easy to work as green wood, but it's good in a pinch.

I had even more luck when using kiln-dried wood for the other parts of the chair besides the sticks. I used kiln-dried white oak with great success to make legs and stretchers. Poplar from the lumberyard made an excellent and easily worked seat.

Cheating the Seat: Alternative Hand Tools

Many woodworkers are put off by "saddling" the seat, which is where you scoop out the wood to make things more comfortable. Traditional bodgers hew the seat with an adze, then finish it with some combination of inshave, travisher, compass plane, scrapers and sandpaper.

I wanted to see if it could be done well with fewer tools.

So I skipped the adze and began the work with the inshave, a tool that resembles a drawknife with a curved blade. Working across the grain, the tool was quick. After hogging out most of the seat, I then worked with the grain to tune things up a bit more.

Cleaning up the tool marks left by the inshave is usually a job for a travisher. One option is to use a chairmaker's curved rasp. These tools resemble overgrown rifflers and can smooth out just about any part of the seat. The French rasps shown in the bottom left photo are from Auriou and are the sweetest rasps I've ever used.

If you're comfortable with handplanes, a curved-sole plane can saddle a seat. The vintage Stanley No. 100½ model makers' plane has a sole that curves both front to back and side to side.

— *Christopher Schwarz*

Saddling With a Grinder

As a maker of traditional Welsh chairs, I like to use traditional tools. But there are times when I have a huge order with a short deadline, or a chairmaking workshop where I have to supply 12 students with roughed-out seats so they can finish their chairs within six days. So I cheat!

Traditionally I use an adze to rough out the shape, a travisher to smooth the adze marks and a devil (a cabinet scraper in a wooden body) to smooth the travisher cuts. The chamfer on the underside is cut with the adze and cleaned up with a spokeshave. By the end of the day my forearms are bulging like Popeye and I have to shake them out to get the feeling back in them.

When in a press, though, I use an Arbortech Pro Industrial Woodcarver – a metal disk with three carbide teeth. After the Arbortech, I use tungsten carbide discs made by Kutzall, which come in three grits and two profiles, to fair out the marks left by the Arbortech. The final surfacing is done with 2" Velcro sanding disks on a foam-backed wheel. I begin with #80 grit and progress to #280 grit.

When all is said and done, the noise, dust and vibration send me back to the adze, travisher and devil. The surface is crisper and the pleasure of hearing myself think make up for the labor.

— *Don Weber, a bodger and blacksmith in Paint Lick, Kentucky*

An Easy-to-Make Travisher

In the world of hand tools, many classic designs came from a world with material, manufacturing and knowledge (or Guild) limitations. Today, we are free to experiment thanks to new tools and technology. Thus when faced with the need to make a travisher, I decided to try a new way.

I love the sweeping shape of the classic travisher, but I've also seen many with split handles and cracked throats. Plus I'm not keen on making heirloom tools. Don't get me wrong, I lust for those curly maple and bubinga beauties, but my goal with this travisher was to get a curved blade to quickly and reliably scoop out seats. The pretty version would have to wait.

I call my design a "moose-eared"

Curved rasps are great for many parts of the chair, from removing tearout in a seat to shaping the outside of the seat, the bow and the comb. Their strength is they can detail curves and work (in general) without regard to grain direction.

The Stanley No. 100½ might not look like much, but its scarcity (and utility) make it a hard plane to find. New adaptations of this tool are available for less money (I paid $80 for my vintage one. Ouch).

Traditionally, the inshave is used after the seat is roughed out with an adze. But my experiments found that the seat can be roughed out by an inshave alone. It takes a little more time, but is a good option until you find (or can afford) a proper adze.

When in a hurry, the Arbortech Pro Industrial Woodcarver is like an electric adze.

After the Arbortech, I clean up my work with these abrasive wheels, which come in different grits.

The final step to smoothing the seat is to fair out the saddle with sandpaper stuck to a foam pad, which will follow the seat's complex contours.

travisher in honor of that famous Minnesotan from Frostbite Falls. It is adaptable to any blade. My tool makes two departures from traditional designs.

First, the toe in front of the blade is a separate piece of wood. This allows me to choose the toe length I want, to contour it to the blade, to add shims behind it to open or close the throat and to easily replace it when it wears.

The second departure is the moose-ear shape. I like to push my travishers, and the ears let me extend my fingers and comfortably apply force through my thumbs. I find it to be ergonomically a better design, and with a traditional sweep under the ears, I can still cup it in my hands like a traditional travisher and pull.

Fabrication is straightforward. Begin with rectangular stock and mark out where the mortises should go to accommodate the blade's tangs. Aligning the cutting edge of the travisher blade with the front of the stock locates where the back edge of the tang will go. Mark the location and add about $1/8$" to allow for throat clearance and a recess for the toe. Using a mortising attachment in my drill press, I cut "square holes" that are centered on the tangs with their backs aligned to my layout marks.

Next, lay out and cut the shallow recess for the toe piece. Drop the blade in its mortises and bottom it onto the stock. Mark the ends of the blade and remove it. I add another $1/16$" of width to each mark and carry these marks around to the front of the stock perpendicular to the bottom edge. Cut an $1/8$"-deep dado between the lines. This dado will hold the toe piece. I cut $1/2$" stock for the toe piece that fits in the groove and is the width of the stock plus approximately $3/4$".

Cutting the throat of the tool – a ramp from the front to the back of the stock – is easy on this design. The ramp begins at the front and ends at the back, where it is $1/2$" deep. Using a chisel and saw, clean out the throat from the front edge to the pencil cut line on the back. Now install

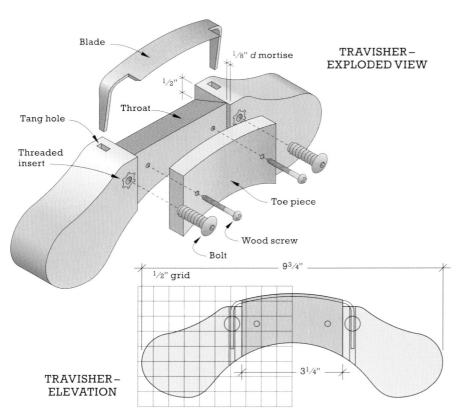

TRAVISHER – EXPLODED VIEW

Blade

$1/8$" *d* mortise

$1/2$"

Throat

Tang hole

Threaded insert

Toe piece

Wood screw

Bolt

TRAVISHER – ELEVATION

$1/2$" grid

$9 3/4$"

$3 1/4$"

This travisher design is easier to make than the traditional version and allows you to shape the toe piece of the tool to suit your work.

the bolts to secure the blade. I use bolts with threaded inserts, which is a reliable and durable system.

Drop the toe piece into its dado with its extra width extending over the blade. Secure it with two screws. Use the blade's edge to scribe a line on the toe piece. Remove the toe piece and cut up to the line. Round the front of the toe piece and reinstall it on the travisher's body.

Mark the moose ear profile on the assembled travisher, remove the blade and head to the band saw. Cut out the shape and then rasp, sand and trim to the desired final shape. Remove the toe piece

This simple but effective jig holds my auger bit at just the right angle. With its assistance, it's hard to miss your mark or stray.

and slide a shim under it and reinstall. Put in the blade and back it out for the depth of cut you want.

With a little tuning, I think you will find that this is a fun travisher to use and modify to your personal preference.
— *Eric Hedberg, a chairmaker and woodworker in St. Paul, Minnesota*

Cheating the Drilling: Perfect Holes for the Legs

The geometry of the leg angles is tough to wrap your brain around. It's a compound angle, and chairmakers have come up with many ways to jig it up.

Once you decide what angles you would like your legs to be, this jig makes it simple.

In essence, it's an oversized doweling jig. Your auger bit is guided by 1" pipe (that's the interior dimension). The pipe is positioned on 2×4s that have a V-groove plowed down the middle and have been trimmed to the correct angle. The pipe is secured to the 2×4s with pipe-hanging straps and screws. The 2×4s are screwed to the plywood top. And cleats around the bottom of the plywood hold the seat blank.

It works like a charm. The only downside to the jig is that it cannot be adjusted to make holes at other angles. Once you build it, you're set. If you want a different set of leg angles, you'll have to build another jig.

Straight Shooter: The Best Way to Drill Spindle Holes

As a boy my father told me stories of my Swedish great-grandfather. An expert marksman, he would line up flat-lain bottle caps along the edge of my grandmother's favorite bench and shoot them off to the delight of my dad and the chagrin of my grandmother. Unfortunately, I learned early that the marksman's eye is not a dominant gene, and that I would be relegated to a life of glasses, odd squinting and creative jigging.

As ancient legend and popular mythology goes, the bodger eyes his target, grabs his brace and augers deftly and accurately from point to point. I believe this is often true, but I also believe that paint covers a multitude of sins. So, when faced with drilling through the arm of my first Welsh stick chair into the seat, I stood back and pondered the consequences. I could argue the virtue of the quaint variations that would occur or I could realize my marksman-eyed spouse would be forever querying me as to whether that was intentional or not.

After some thought, I came up with a fixture that I call a straight-shooter joystick. Like all fixtures in my shop it is borne of necessity and assembled out of the scraps piled under my miter saw.

The heart of the joystick is two blocks of wood. The bottom block holds a partial wood sphere, and the top block is drilled straight through to hold a drill-

Here's a close look at the section of the jig that guides the drill bit into the bow of the chair. The location of the bushing is locked in place by the T-nut and knob. The bushing is sized to your drill bit, ⅝" in this case.

The hemisphere is placed in a countersink in the seat while you drill the hole in the chair's bow.

You cannot miss with this hole-boring jig and you never have to figure out any angles. Clamp the bow in place and place the jig in a small countersunk hole on the spindle deck. Put your drill bit in the bushing and fire away.

The Veritas Dowel Maker will turn any species of wood into a dowel. Setting up the jig takes some time and can be frustrating, but the results are good.

ing sleeve, both located exactly the same distance from their mounting edge. Attached to the stick, their common offset centerline lets me shoot a straight line from the seat to the arm.

Using the device is straightforward: The spindle locations are located on the seat and a small countersink is used to create a small cone-shaped depression at each location. I clamp the arm into place above the seat and mark in pencil the corresponding through-points for the spindles in the arms. I place the hemisphere of the joystick in the selected location on the seat and then, with a brad point bit in the sleeve, locate the bit on the corresponding pencil mark. A touch of the trigger quickly makes a hole through the arm. Next I take a drill bit extender with a ⅝"-hardwood sleeve bearing and slide the extender through the ⅝" hole. The hardwood sleeve is then fit snugly in the spindle hole of the arm. I attach my bit to the extender's end, align it with the location in the seat and drill away.

The system is quick. If you make an

MDF template for the seat with pre-drilled-to-size spindle locations, you can make quick "production" runs. When I use a template, I bore my seat spindle holes with a Forstner bit. It rides on the edges of the template hole and creates nice, clean holes.

One shortcoming with this system is the spindles themselves. Variations in the spindles can make dry assembly a little frustrating, but because of the accuracy of the holes it is straightforward to find the rogue spindle and make the appropriate adjustments.

Cheating the Spindles: Avoid Turning & Shaving

Getting your spindles to a round shape can be a challenge without a lathe. You can spokeshave them, but that can be time-consuming and requires a bit of skill.

Luckily, there are a couple good jigs. They cost a bit, but they're cheaper than a new lathe.

The Veritas Dowel Maker is an ingenious jig that turns square stock into a

dowel. A socket in your drill turns the stock as it passes two knives – one to rough out the shape and the second to shave it to perfect thickness. You can adjust the jig in tiny increments to get just the right size.

While the jig works well, it has a couple drawbacks. It requires a lot of little adjustments to get the device working just so. It's not particularly complicated, but it is time-consuming to learn. The second drawback is the price. The basic unit costs $199 and cuts only 1"- and ¹⁵⁄₁₆"-diameter dowels. To cut other common chairmaking sizes (½", ⅝" and ¾") you will need to purchase almost $130 of additional tooling.

The other option is to buy rounding planes. I use a sled that is made of two pieces of scrap and a wooden guide that fits in the miter track of my band saw. It is super simple to make. First, glue the two pieces of scrap together to make an "L" about 8" long. Next, pencil a line on the guide that will hold it 4° clockwise to the blade. Carefully glue the "L" onto the guide, aligning the back edge with the pencil line. Allow the "L" to extend past the band saw's blade. A couple of short brads ensure the "L" won't come off the guide.

When all is dry, pass the sled through the blade and cut off the end. To use, take your "squared" wedge stock, put it in the sled and cut. Reverse the stock, aligning the wedge "point" near the edge of the sled. Cut again and you have a perfect 8° wedge.

For Shaving Spindles, Meet the Shaving Pony

Several years ago a few upstate New York members of an online mailing list for hand-tool enthusiasts got together to enjoy a picnic, share toys and admire each other's work. One brought a Windsor chair she'd built at Michael Dunbar's school, The Windsor Institute. It was the first time we'd seen a hand-built Windsor. The comfort and beauty of the design was impressive, and it was much nicer than a machine-made replica.

We decided as a group to build Windsor chairs using the techniques

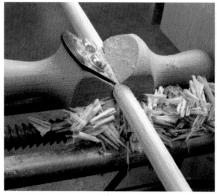
This rounding plane by Ray Iles excels at turning down your sticks to the right dimension.

This simple three-piece band saw jig will cut perfect wedges all day long.

described in Dunbar's book. This group approach gave us the opportunity to share our skills, learn from each other's mistakes and pool our tools.

Handmade Windsor chairs are noteworthy for their spindle construction, each split down the grain and then shaped with a drawknife and spokeshave. This gives them strength and flexibility that turned spindles lack, along with the facets that give character to a

The shaving pony allows you to work chair spindles without a space-sucking shaving horse. This simple jig clamps in your bench vise and stores away in a corner or on the wall when not in use.

handmade chair. Traditionally, a large shaving horse would be employed to do this. The horse permits the blank to be clamped firmly yet turned repeatedly as it is shaved round. None of us had a shaving horse. No one had the space to store one or access to the timbers required to build a traditional horse. We tried to use vises and clamps to shave spindles at the bench, but it didn't work.

We needed something small enough for the group sessions and easy to build from common and inexpensive materials.

A shaving horse uses a moving head that comes down on a fixed plate attached to a bench to clamp the workpiece. A foot pedal attached to the head allows the worker to apply and release pressure quickly. The fixed plate could be held in the bench vise, with a foot pedal to apply clamping pressure. Offsetting the pivot points of the clamp would improve the clamping action.

So one night Dave Matthews devised a prototype that did all this out of a 2×4, some drywall screws, and a couple of bolts. It was simple and it worked. Robb Young fleshed it out with uprights supporting each side of the jig, removable dowels and adjustable jaws to better grip different blank thicknesses. Now we could sit or stand right at the workbench and shave away. Our group christened it the "shaving pony."

The "shaving pony" is easy to make from construction lumber, a couple of hardwood dowels and screws. The dimensions shown in the illustration seem comfortable for work at a 34"-high

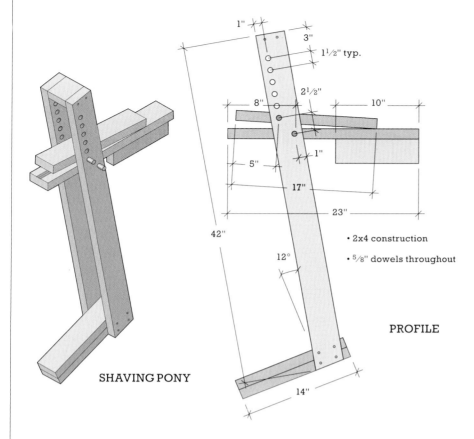

1"

3"

1½" typ.

2½"

8"

10"

1"

5"

17"

23"

42"

12°

• 2x4 construction

• ⅝" dowels throughout

PROFILE

14"

SHAVING PONY

Supplies & Resources

Tools for Working Wood
toolsforworkingwood.com or
800-426-4613

• Auriou chairmaker's curving riffler
  rasp, #AU-RR06.XX, $82.95 (10")

• Ray Iles rounding planes, available
  in a variety of sizes, #MS-IROUND.
  XX, $65.95 to $68.95

Lee Valley Tools
leevalley.com or 800-871-8158

• Veritas Dowel Maker,
  #05J45.01, $199

Additional inserts available,
priced at $42.50 ea.

• Veritas Power Tenon Cutters, available in sizes from ⅝" to 2" diameter.
  Priced between $90 to $115 ea.

Woodcraft
woodcraft.com or 800-225-1153

• Arbortech Pro Industrial
  Woodcarver, item #128258, $164.99

The Country Workshops
countryworkshops.org or
828-656-2280

• *The Chairmaker's Workshop*
  (author's reprint edition), $50

Windsor Chair Resources
windsorchairresources.com

• An online treasure trove of sources
  for tools, hints from chairmakers and
  lists of chairmakers across the country. An essential bookmark for every
  bodger's browser.

Prices as of publication date.

bench, but can be modified. Softwood is best, so the jaws won't mar your work and the uprights will grab the dowels. Screw the parts together.

Use the drawing as a guide for construction. Each shaving pony is a bit different depending on the height of the bench, the materials available and what you want to clamp. The pony shown in the drawing will accommodate bigger stock, including a chair's crest rail. If you are merely shaving spindles the uprights can be considerably shorter, more like 34".

First, cut all your pieces to size. Sandwich the uprights together, temporarily clamp them and drill ⅝" holes through the pieces in the locations shown. Cut the bottom ends of the uprights at about a 10° or 12° angle down toward the front.

Make the pedal by gluing the two foot pieces together face to face. Now make the jaws. Cut a few lengthwise grooves about ⅛" deep in the middle inch of the inside faces of both jaws. These grooves help hold your blank tight.

Drill ⅝"-diameter holes through the jaws in the locations shown. These will

secure the jaws to the rest of the pony.

Add a support block to the lower jaw that will allow you to clamp the shaving pony in your vise. The size and location of this block will depend on your vise and where it is on your workbench. The object is to clamp it firmly while allowing as much of the lower jaw as possible to rest on the vise and benchtop for stability.

Now assemble the shaving pony. Screw and glue the pedal between the uprights at the proper angle. Then do the same to the top piece. Put the lower jaw in place and secure it with one dowel through the jaws. This will allow the pony to pivot but keep the jaw between the uprights. The upper jaw is secured by the other dowel, which will allow you to move the jaw to a higher or lower position. Add a knob to the end of each dowel to make them easy to remove.

To use the shaving pony, clamp it into your bench vise with the pedal facing you. Locate the upper jaw with its dowel through one of the upper pairs of holes, leaving just enough space between the jaws to accept your blank. Stepping on the pedal clamps your work firmly, but it can easily be shifted just by lifting your foot.

This shaving pony can be as stylish as you wish, but we'd save our energy for shaving all those chair spindles!

— Dave Matthews and Robb Young are amateur woodworkers in Retsof and Pittsford, New York. (Thanks to Esther Heller and Tim Fuss.)

18th-Century Chairmaking

BY ADAM CHERUBINI

I'm going to turn my attention to chairmaking for a while. I've been hesitant to make chairs because they are fairly difficult to build, and frankly, I didn't feel I was up to the task. Joint quality is much more important in chairs than casework. If 80 percent of my dovetails are tight, my carcase will be fine. But if a chair has 20 percent of its joints loose, it's going to fail.

To make matters worse, chair joints are often not perpendicular to their reference faces or to other joints. I have been getting away with fairly crude stock preparation and in some instances, marking and measuring. A cabinetmaker can often simply mark one piece directly from its mate. You generally can't do that with chairs. Parts are built up individually and joined later.

I think I've had good reasons to shy away from chairmaking. But I've decided to face my chair phobia head on. I'm going to start with a relatively simple chair and work up from there. My goal is to acquire skills, not chairs. I'm hoping this pursuit will make me a better woodworker.

A Common Chair

There were a variety of seating forms in the 18th century, from stools to chairs to upholstered pieces. Early 18th-century documents include what we call "ladderback" chairs more often, and in greater numbers, than any other form of seating furniture. Sorry Windsor chairmakers – these uncomfortable, structurally marginal chairs were the ubiquitous seating of the 18th century. The basic frames were made with great speed. One late 17th-century source indicates a chairmaker's apprentice could build two-and-a-half frames per day. Seats could be woven at a rate of nine per day.

Primarily identified by their seating material (flagg, straw or rush bottomed), ladderbacks' exact appearance can't always be linked to specific documents. Backs may have been comprised of vertical spindles or horizontal slats. Legs and backs may have been decoratively turned or simply riven and shaved. What we do know is that many have survived to our time. They were made from a range of domestic hardwoods and were almost always painted. Surviving chairs feature straightforward construction; turned posts are joined to turned stretchers with cylindrical tenons. The mortises are, of course, holes. X-rays show round-bottomed holes – the telltale sign of the use of spoon bits.

I suspect all of us have sat in ladderback chairs at least once in our lives. Simple to make, these chairs were reproduced in great numbers by chair factories in the 19th and 20th centuries. These factory-made chairs, undoubtedly the very chairs many of us experienced, are generally unsatisfying. Their loose joints and uncomfortable backs may be contributors to the undeserved bad reputation these chairs have gotten. I'm not saying this will be the chair you'll seek out for A&E television's six-hour presenta-

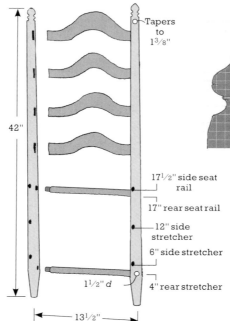

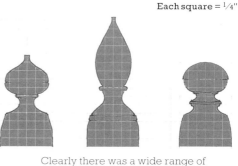

Each square = ¼"

42"

Tapers to 1³⁄₈"

17¹⁄₂" side seat rail

17" rear seat rail

12" side stretcher

6" side stretcher

1¹⁄₂" d

4" rear stretcher

13¹⁄₂"

I discuss the slat spacing in the text, but you can start making your story pole with this diagram.

Clearly there was a wide range of shapes turned into the tops of 18th-century chairs. This is an area where you can express your taste and show off your turning ability all at the same time! The grid shown is ¹⁄₄". I thought I saw finials turned down to a ¹⁄₂" diameter or less. On the next set I build, I'll try to be more aggressive with my gouge.

tion of "Pride and Prejudice." But I can't help but wonder how good these chairs can be if they are carefully and faithfully reproduced.

Stock Prep

Period stock preparation for chairs like these would probably have involved riv-

ing all of the components from logs. I suspect the legs would have been made by splitting a small log into quarters, then using a froe to rive roughly 2" × 2" pieces. I didn't have a log long enough for this project, so I began with 8/4 S2S soft maple. Kiln-dried maple is more difficult to turn and bore with a spoon bit than is green wood. It's also important to ensure that the grain is very straight or the finished leg will not remain so. Its dryness necessitates even tighter joint quality, as we can't expect the posts to shrink around the tenons. That said,

I'm cutting the slat mortises for two chairs. I suspect period chairmakers would have used more mass production techniques than cabinetmakers due to the repetitive nature of their work.

I wanted to try spring-pole lathe turning, but didn't want to spend a lot of time carefully constructing stiff ways and poppets. I found my electric wood lathe had nearly everything I needed in a spring pole lathe – a stiff bed, adjustable tailstock and a tool rest. So I screwed an 8' long red oak 1×2 to the ceiling and tied some scrap leather to it. I passed the knotted leather strap down to a scrap of pine on the floor. I won't be demonstrating at shows with this lathe, but it's been sufficient to learn on.

commercial boards can be used successfully, though they are clearly disadvantageous. I sawed my boards into squares, following the grain rather than the edge of the board.

I cut the mortises for the back slats before turning the legs. I cut them in my usual fashion, but intuition tells me period chairmakers probably bored a series of holes with a small spoon bit after the leg was turned. If you decide to mortise before turning as I did, make sure you choose centers in line with the mortises. If you are starting with riven stock, you may choose against mortising first.

Pole Lathe Turning

Documentary evidence suggests period chairmakers could turn out chair parts very quickly. Period images suggest they used spring pole lathes. I've found spring-pole lathe turning to be both rewarding and challenging. You can forget about going straight from the grinder to the lathe, for example. Your turning

gouges must be as sharp as any other chisel in your shop. Scraping generally doesn't work well. Unlike a treadle lathe, the spring pole lathe's belt transmits torque well. The workpiece doesn't slip forgivingly when you do something wrong. If you're not careful, you can get catches on the return stroke (the workpiece spins forward and backward with each tread). Make too many mistakes and your center will become oval. But using a light touch, a sharp tool and careful technique, the spring pole is capable of fast and beautiful work.

Boring

The spoon bit can be difficult to start at a precise location. I found a little more down force helped. You can also cheat by boring a starter hole with a center bit. I've heard of guys using a gouge to make a dimple in the round leg as a starting place for the spoon. My take is that this is one of those things you must simply practice. Keep in mind that boring a precise hole in a scrap pine board is different than boring a hole in the center of a hardwood dowel.

Slats

The backs of this sort of chair feature carefully scrolled slats, bent into a comfortable, curved shape. I've not seen an 18th-century chair with flat slats, either unformed or unscrolled.

Rarely are the slats identical top to bottom. Sometimes the top slat is slightly larger than the others. I think these slat designs were quite carefully considered. I don't believe these were done thoughtlessly. The graduated slats create an exaggerated perspective that juxtaposes the

tapering of the legs and detailing of the front legs, which I believe sought to correct a standing observer's perspective of the chair.

I want to leave you with two thoughts: First, this shape is really important artistically. If you want to capture the period, look carefully at as many chairs as possible, preferably in the flesh. I prefer to bring a sketch pad and draw them right there. Back in the shop, mock up a half-dozen sets in cardboard before you cut any wood. Take your time and get this the way you want it. It's important.

Second, the slats on period chairs are fairly thin, rarely more than $1/4$". And the oxbow shape is an effective torsion spring. I hinted earlier about how uncomfortable these straight-backed chairs are. Well this design introduces a little flex, which I've found helpful. I can't help but think this was deliberate.

Period chairmakers probably didn't make steam boxes to bend chair slats. I was told they simply boiled parts like these, so that's what I did. You may find success bending straight-grained, kiln-dried, flat-sawn stock. The curvature is subtle. I had some success with test pieces. My advice is to try it before you decide it's impossible. For this chair, I had some green white oak lying around so I used that. I split out pieces on the medullary rays with a froe. Don't bother trying to flatten these pieces with a handplane. Bring them smooth and to a uniform $1/4$" thickness (depending on your mortise chisel's width) using a drawknife. Thick areas won't bend as readily as thin. So uniformity of thickness is important in achieving a smooth formed curve.

Shape the slats with a turning or cop-

I'm smart. I use my head! Windsor chairmakers don't need this crutch technique. But steadying the top of the brace (wimble) with my noggin helps me to bore straight holes. A piece of scrap in a slat mortise helped me to set the angle. This angle is 30°, which proved too much for large people.

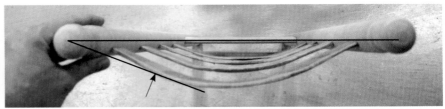

The mortise angle for chairs like these should be between 20° and 30°. Choosing the correct angle can be difficult. Dozens of people sat in one of my chairs at a recent furniture show. Some were comfortable. Some were not. Smaller people with smaller rib cages (women in particular) were more comfortable with a greater curvature to the slats, describing the chair as "cozy." Larger folks preferred flatter slats. I would build a chair to accommodate the size of the sitters if I could. Otherwise, less curvature seems to hold a slight advantage for the wider public.

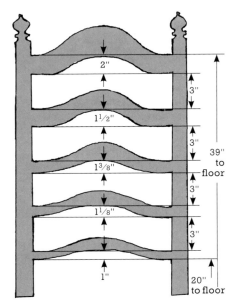

The diagram shows measurements: 2", 3", 1½", 3", 1⅜", 39" to floor, 3", 1⅛", 3", 1", 20" to floor

I examined many chairs before making my own. The various shapes of their back slats fascinated me. This oxbow shape appealed to me most. Each slat appeared to be twice as high as its tenon. The tenons increased in size from 1" to about 2". On no chair was the topmost slat higher than the legs. I also noticed the spaces between the slats were equal.

Make a chair from a what? That's right: Dowels from the local home center store. My chief concern building this sort of chair was the joinery. So I bought dowels and made a practice chair from them. I couldn't find dowels bigger than 1⅛". That threw off my design a little. And dowels aren't cheap. But there is a rack full of them at the store and I felt this was a cheap education.

ing saw and smooth the saw cuts with a spokeshave or rasp. Test fit the slats into the mortises in the chair back. Mark a line on the slat indicating the depth of penetration into the leg. When you later bend the slats in place, you can use this line to ensure the slat has reached the mortise's full depth. So just let me be clear: I shaped the slats first, then bent them. I don't know if this is how it was done in the period.

Insert the wet, hot slats into the mortises. The lower stretchers have already been fitted and glued with hot hide glue. Clamp or tie the tops of the legs together to prevent them from spreading. Check that the slats are fully inserted using the line you drew earlier. If the slats aren't perfectly aligned you may be able to force them into shape with clamps while they are still hot.

How This Species Survives
The basic structure of these chairs consists of turned legs, rails and stretchers. Legs are bored to receive the rails and stretchers. The ends of the rails and stretchers are turned down to form ten-

ons. Crisp shoulders help ensure tenons reach full depth during assembly. The parts are glued together with hot hide glue. This may be an important design feature. These chairs do tend to come apart with age. A reversible glue, a glue that can be reactivated with more of the same, a glue with some gap filling properties, may be the key to these chairs' long-term survival.

Why the Fronts are Fancy
There are a variety of different styles of leg and front stretcher turnings. In general, I think these chairs were stored against the walls of the home, not tucked around a dining table, so chair fronts were visible and an obvious location to add ornamentation. Delaware Valley chairs often exhibit exaggerated and bulbous versions of the front stretcher. Leg turnings are fairly simple, featuring beads and coves with a little vase on top. Interestingly, very similar leg turnings would find their way onto Philadelphia's first Windsor chairs. Likewise, the way the front legs tenon into the front seat rail reminds me of a Windsor chair. I usually

think of the Windsor chair as a highly innovative and revolutionary (forgive the pun) furniture form. But I think this design suggests that Windsor chairmakers were influenced by earlier pieces just like everybody else.

Building the Front
In my observation of period chairs, it appeared the side stretchers were always parallel to the floor. So I used those measurements for the front legs. I placed a bead and cove 1" above each of the side stretchers. The tops of the front legs featured a shouldered tenon. I was curious if these were ever tapered like Windsor chair seats. I haven't seen any evidence of that yet. So make them cylindrical like all the others.

The front center stretcher was turned next. Its overall length was about 18". This length allowed 1¼"-long tenons. I determined the shoulder-to-shoulder

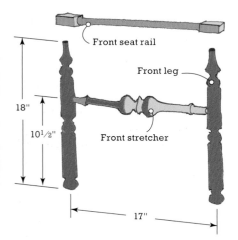

Front seat rail

Front leg

Front stretcher

18"

10½"

17"

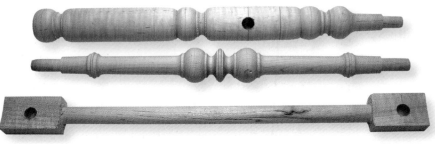

The front legs (top), front stretcher (middle), and front seat rail (bottom) are ready for assembly. Tenons have been turned but their ends will need to be rounded to clear the round-bottomed hole left by the spoon bit. The rectangular sections on the ends of the seat rail are called pommels.

The basic joinery is not difficult. I chose a slightly more complicated version, however. In the diagram above, notice that the legs tenon into the front seat rail from underneath. This is not the most typical design. Generally the seat rails all tenon into the front leg, which then protrudes slightly above the seat. I chose this design because I thought it looked a little more refined, and I enjoy mixing refined features with cruder elements or textures.

dimension by subtracting the leg diameter (approximately 1½") from 17" (a dimension that I got from measuring numerous period chairs).

The front seat rail was next. I sawed out a piece of maple 1" thick × 1½" wide × 19½" long. I purposely left it long so I could saw off the lathe centers and trim it nicely to the seat's shape. The leg positions were marked and locations of the pommels were established. Then it was

back to the lathe to turn down the portion between the pommels.

Joint Quality: Not Too Tight

With all four parts done, I glued up the chair front and set it aside. Concerned about joint integrity, I first made very tight-fitting tenons. My tenons were so tight that I needed to twist the parts to get them in. This proved too tight for hide glue. The hot glue either swelled the wood or was too grabby to allow assembly of the parts.

Make sure you turn your tenons so that they can be installed with just hand pressure, pushing straight in. Tenons dry-fit this way will probably need the help of a mallet to go together with hide glue. I also think it's important to fit the tenons and glue them up in one day.

One more trick: Determining the overall length of the rails and stretchers isn't just about ensuring maximum tenon length or being frugal with your material. When the turning stock is at its full length, the lathe centers are preserved in the finished piece. This allows you to

With the front and back of the chair completed, all I have to do is join them together. Getting the angles and locations correct is simple if you are careful.

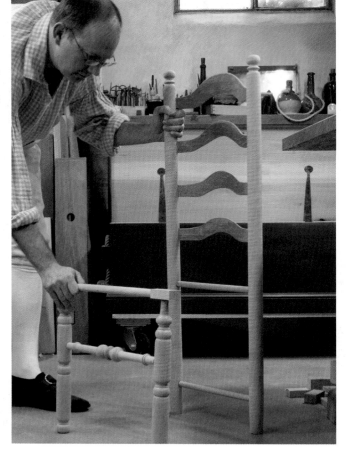

I don't think the size of the pommel matters. Do whatever looks good to you. I marked in from the centerline of the leg about 1¼". I trimmed the outside edge just a little proud of the rush.

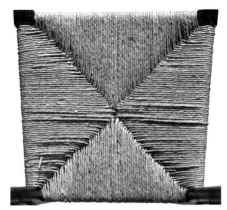

I measured a number of chairs. Back legs were often no more than 13–14" apart. The depths of the seats were often 16" or more. I found this a bit surprising. I thought the seats would be shallower. I think a longer seat makes a chair a bit more comfortable to slouch in. The distance between the front legs was about 17".

turn down a tenon that's just a little too fat or trim away a shoulder to make the fit just right. The alternative is you saw off the lathe centers prior to dry fit and find some other way to take a uniform $1/32$" off a tenon. Some guys sand their tenons. But the lathe is just so much easier for this sort of work.

As cabinetmakers, we develop dimen-sions (or not), mark them on our work, then cut to the line. But this chairmaking is different. The dimensions are used to derive what we really need – angles to set our bevel gauge to guide the boring of holes, and overall lengths and shoulder-to-shoulder dimensions for the rails and stretchers. We can find all this math-ematically, but I prefer to simply draw it out full size, then use the drawing to mark the parts.

Intersecting Tenons?

The need to create a somewhat flat seat necessitates some compromise at the seat rail connections. You have two choices: You can either make the tenons short enough so that they don't intersect (like a cabinetmaker would) or you can allow a small $1/2$" offset between the rails and intersect their tenons. The former approach would probably result in a weak chair. The latter is what was typi-cally done.

I think the forces acting on a chair are front to back (introduced at the seat, reacted at the floor). This causes rack-ing at the side seat rails and stretchers. Because of this, I think you need very good joint quality at these locations. This also tells me that, given the choice, it's

wiser to compromise the front and rear seat rails and let the sides remain whole. Sorry if this is too technical. Our ances-tors probably had a century of practical experience informing such decisions. In my case, keeping the side rails and stretchers as strong as possible deter-mined my assembly sequence. I built up the front and back of the chair. I laid each flat on the bench, then bored the angled holes for the side pieces.

With all the holes bored, I did a test fit (always a good idea). I tried to rotate each of the rungs. Any rail or stretcher that would not budge went back to the lathe. I guess I'm accustomed to working with hot hide glue because the glue-up was uneventful. You brush on the glue and put the chair together.

Wrapping it Up

There's primary source evidence that these chair were painted a wide variety of colors. Black was fairly common, so I chose that. I tried my standard recipe of milk paint followed by oil and wax. That looked pretty good. But I also tried a semi-gloss rust preventative (hint hint) enamel thinking it would be closer to the originals' shiny oil finish. Frankly, both finishes looked fine and the enamel was

You could make a scaled or full-sized drawing, or a template to help you build your chair. But I prefer to do what Kaare Loftheim does in Colonial Williamsburg's Cabinetshop. I lay out the dimensions on my work bench top. Your bench top is a convenient place for proj-ect plans and they are harder to lose. I'm guessing many of you won't take this advice! And I just planed this bench!

I've got the front built up and you can see I've scribed the leg's centerline onto the back of the seat rail. Positioning the rail carefully, I see that the side rail must be inset if its centerline is to intersect the leg's centerline. If you've followed me, that's it. This is as tricky as it gets. I've made a mark indicating where I must start the hole for the side stretcher. All I need to do now is bore the right angles in the right spots.

I'm boring the hole in the back of the front seat rail for the side seat rail. The distance between these stretchers is just enough for me to swing my brace. I like having the stretchers in place so I can check the angle of the hole I'm boring. Photos are cruel masters. Looks like the first hole I bored was good and the successive holes stand up a little bit. I'd like to say this isn't a problem. But I may have to make the other side similar and force the seat rails the same amount on both sides to fit the chair back.

easier. So I chose that.

I promised I would show you how to weave the seat. I have to break that promise. I used a commercially available, pre-twisted, natural sea grass rush. I needed 2½ rolls and the process took about three hours. A 17th-century document indicates seats could be woven at a rate of nine per day. Obviously, they knew something I don't. Turns out there are many different ways of weaving a seat and twice as many different materials. If I come up with something you can't find online, I'll post it to my blog.

Small Changes; Big Differences

I feel I can be brutally honest with you: I'm not crazy about this chair. There's too much curvature in the back slats for me to be comfortable. I chose a 30° mortise angle, which, in retrospect is too high for someone my size. I designed a five-slat chair, but built a four-slat chair to save time riving, shaving and forming. That was a big mistake. The slats are just too far apart. I think the legs are too thick. I should have turned them down another ⅛" and added more taper. And yes, I think an ⅛" really does make a noticeable difference. And the front stretcher should be 50 percent larger in diameter.

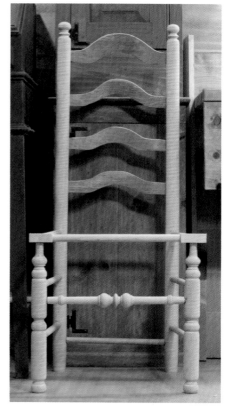

Tight-fitting joints leave no room for error. Force a stretcher into a hole, and the chair can rack out of shape. I expect experience will teach me how to deal with problems like this one in more elegant ways. I chose to let the rear stretcher be where it wanted to be and introduce no weird internal stresses. It's very obvious in this view, but much less so in every other.

Overall, I think the chair just lacks a certain pop.

I focused this project on the process, exploring the joinery in particular. In that, I was successful. I bored good holes. Turned good tenons. Built strong chairs. I prepared my tools carefully and practiced my technique. But if what I make isn't beautiful, isn't comfortable, its tight joinery ceases to be a virtue.

Spoon Bits

Spoon bits are tricky to use. These old flat-tang bits had to be carefully mounted in bit "pads." It's important to note that the flat tang is not centered with the bit, but off to one side. New, square-tang bits don't have this problem. For this sort of chair, a ⅝" bit is required and possibly a small one, maybe ¼" (or less) for pegs or boring holes for the slat mortises. The advantages of the spoon bit are that it's easy to change its direction, allowing fairly fine adjustment of the angle of a hole during drilling, and its round bottom. This feature lets you bore almost through a post, providing for maximum tenon length. One thing to watch for when using a spoon bit is that they don't eject chips. So you can be cranking away waiting to see some progress only to find you've bored too deep a hole. Check your hole depth frequently.

Fast Fix for Teetering Legs

BY GARY ROGOWSKI

Rock-n-roll. That's what four-legged pieces have a habit of doing – even with perfect joinery and a careful and unhurried assembly. Even with all the care and attention you paid to building it correctly, it doesn't sit flat on your floor but moves back and forth rocking on two legs. What gives?

Don't worry; it's just life at the bench and Euclidean geometry raising its head again. If you build everything with three legs, you won't have this problem. But because a lot of tables and chairs have four legs, you are constantly faced with this issue. Just a little pull from one of the joints and your chair or table doesn't sit flat. The legs are still the same length but they're pulled out of true or flat by your assembly.

The Problem

Let's say you need to remove a bit of length from one or two legs. As little as a $\frac{1}{32}$" or $\frac{1}{16}$" can be a lot to take off with a handplane, but too little to remove with a saw – even if you could line up your saw perfectly. So, how do you true the legs without either making your chair too short or making yourself frustrated in the process?

Let's understand the problem first. A four-legged chair doesn't sit flat for one of two reasons. It either sits on an uneven floor or the chair itself is twisted. How do you determine where the problem lies? As I tell my students and all my clients, my bench is the Center of the Universe.

Use a table saw as if it were a plane to quickly shave down unstable legs to level a wobbly seat.

This twisted board illustrates just how a four-legged piece can also twist. There are two opposing high sides vs. two low ones. The winding sticks show what's high and low.

Check for twist using the bench as a flat reference surface. Pushing on opposing corners will identify which legs are longer; mark those with chalk.

Truing legs with a block plane requires time and ingenuity to make sure the piece stays stable and doesn't tear out as you attempt to trim it to length.

If it sits flat on my bench, then it's flat. If it moves to the floor and rocks, it's the floor. Of course you could move the piece around until it finds a spot where it's not tipping then never move it, but that's not a reasonable solution. So for all intents and purposes, my bench is my reference surface and sets the standard to which I work. If the piece sits flat on my bench, then it's good to go out the door.

Four-legged pieces can twist for any number of reasons: too much clamping pressure on one side versus the other, mortises cut slightly off center from each other or tenons made at slightly different locations. Little things during construction can add up to small variations that result in a rock so bad in the piece that you think your wood is possessed. (Heck – the boards may actually be possessed and moved or warped as you cut them.) Clearly, this can affect your joinery. Any of these things can add up to a piece that seems to have two longer legs. Even if your legs are equal in length, your task is to trim the bottoms of the seemingly longer ones.

Now you have to make sure you know which leg or legs to trim. A piece rocks because it developed a twist and two legs are pulled up and seem shorter than the other two. It's just like a board that's twisted or a cabinet face that isn't flat. Two opposing corners are high or longer, and two are low or shorter. When adjusting a four-legged piece that's teetering, the first critical mistake you can make is to remove wood from the wrong legs. To determine which legs need adjustment, set the piece on your bench and push down on one pair of opposing legs and then the other. The piece will rock easily when the short legs are pressed. Pushing on the long legs yields no movement. These are the legs to cut. Get this straight in your head and mark the long legs with chalk before making any cuts.

The common solution to adjusting the leg length is to saw the legs off or hand-plane the bottoms of the legs to shorten them. Sawing, if not done exactly right the first time, can lead to a succession of cuts that can render your chair suitable only for the kiddie table.

A second solution is done at the bench using a handplane or rasp, but it's difficult work because you're removing end

Set the blade height for a mere $1/64$" to $1/32$". You should just feel the blade coming up out of the table throat plate insert. A saw blade with a flat-top grind works best.

True a leg on the table saw the quick and easy way. Make sure the blade is set for a very small cut. Laterally move one of the longer legs slowly over the spinning blade.

Check to see if you cut all the way across the bottom of the leg. Sometimes you'll miss the corner of a leg.

grain from the bottoms of the legs. If you don't own or can't sharpen a handplane, it will be slow going. A file or rasp has a tendency to round over the leg. You also have to figure out a way to hold the piece securely while you work on it. You could try belt sanding the long legs but the risks are too great. So what is the answer? Use your table saw instead, but use it as a plane.

The Solution

Now stop gasping. This method works great if your saw table is flat, you set the blade height properly and you are reasonably sure handed. The table saw table acts as your reference surface with the blade shaving off a tiny amount from the bottom of the leg that's too long. To get started, set the table or chair on the table saw table and see if it's rocking the same way

it did on your bench. If not, then one or maybe both of those surfaces aren't true. But if you're getting the same results, proceed with this surefire technique.

If you have a blade with flat-top grind (usually a rip blade) for your saw, put that on because it tends to cut more quickly and create a slightly smoother cut with less tear-out than an alternate-top-bevel blade. Now the key is to set the blade height for about $1/64$" – just enough to feel it coming out of the table. This will be enough to remove some wood but not so much that it creates problems.

When the piece no longer rocks on the saw table, take it to your bench and clean up the leg bottoms with a few quick passes using either a block plane or file. Chamfer the leg's bottom edges then set it on your bench to check again for flat in the center of your universe.

Scoop a Chair Seat

BY MARIO RODRIGUEZ

With a simple, shop-made jig, a table saw can make quick work of scooping a chair seat.

Woodworkers use all sorts of techniques to scoop out their chair seats. Many commonly resort to hacking out the waste with traditional tools such as an adze, travisher and scorp. Others design and assemble elaborate jigs to precisely guide and control a router. Some take the high-tech route and employ CNC equipment. But no woodworkers I know would turn to their table saws to get this tricky job done.

About 20 years ago I stumbled onto a unique scooping method in a self-published book by Robert Marquis titled, *Making the Classic Windsor Chair*. As a chairmaker, I browsed the book and was intrigued by one technique that the author used that was radical, imaginative and maybe even daring. Marquis used the table saw to cut a shallow but symmetrical hollow in his seat blanks.

His technique yielded results that were flatter, less sculpted and had a machine-cut quality. Because I was making more traditional chair styles then, I shelved the book and didn't give it much thought for the next 20 years.

Later I became interested in mid-century furniture designs, particu-larly Scandinavian chairs, and recalled Marquis's unusual method. I was so skeptical of the technique that I consulted a candidate for a doctorate in engineering before attempting it myself. With a green light from the engineer, I constructed the necessary jigs and prepared a couple of seat blanks.

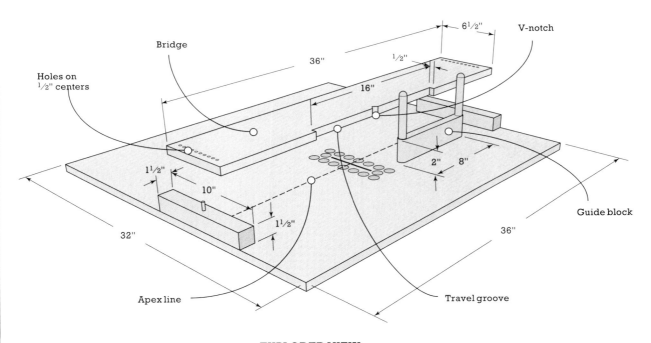

Bridge

Holes on 1/2" centers

6 1/2"

V-notch

36"

1/2"

16"

1 1/2"

10"

1 1/2"

2" 8"

Guide block

32"

36"

Apex line

Travel groove

EXPLODED VIEW

Chair Seat Scooping Jig

NO.	ITEM	T	W	L	MATERIAL
		DIMENSIONS (INCHES)			
1	Base	3/4	36	32	MDF
2	Bridge supports	1 1/2	1 1/2	10	Hardwood
1	Bridge	3/4	6 1/2	36	MDF
1	Guide block	3/4	2	8	Hardwood
2	Guide-block handles	1/2 dia.		4 3/4	Hardwood

Cove Cuts on Steroids

Most woodworkers are familiar with cove mouldings cut using a table saw. You pass material along its length, guided by a fence, diagonally across a raised table saw blade to produce a cove cut. Well, the seat-scooping technique is a variation on that.

Using a jig to guide the work, you pass the material across the raised table saw blade, stop at a given distance, then make a U-turn and return to the starting point. Successive passes expand the width of the scoop. The depth of the scoop is determined by the height setting of the blade. I usually cut to a depth of $1/4$".

The jigs and technique that follow show you how to cut an attractive scoop that measures approximately $14^1/2$" long × $14^1/2$" wide. Both the width and the front-to-back dimensions are reached as cuts are made along the 16" travel groove, and as the bridge portion of the jig is moved forward on successive passes. Each pass increases both measurements of the seat's scoop.

Here's the Scoop

Scooping a chair with this table saw jig isn't as scary as it may seem at first glance. Sure, I was a bit nervous when I first used it – but I quickly learned it really is a safe operation. Best of all, the result is a crisply carved chair seat that is done in little time and requires a minimal amount of sanding. I usually spend no more than 10 to 15 minutes cleaning up the seat blank after the scooping is done. You might wonder what saw blade to use. In my shop, I use a standard combination blade.

Here are the steps to carve seat blanks using the jig:

1. Remove the table saw throat plate to improve dust collection. Clamp the jig base to the saw and raise the blade to $1/8$" above the base.

2. Attach the guide block to the underside of the seat blank. It should be screwed down at the front edge of the seat and centered on its width.

3. Place the bridge on the bridge support blocks. Engage both the right (R) and left (L) holes marked "1" on the bridge with the steel pins on the bridge support blocks.

4. Place the seat blank upside down on the jig base. About half of the blank will be under the bridge. The blank should be positioned to the left of the saw blade with the front edge of the seat facing to the right. Align the guide block with the left stop of the 16"-long travel groove in the bridge.

5. Start the saw and with the blade spinning, carefully and slowly move the guide block along the travel groove from left to right until it

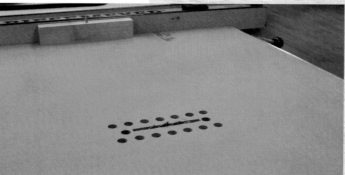

To prepare for scooping, clamp the jig securely to the table saw then raise the saw blade to $1/8$" above the base of the jig.

The guide block is secured to the underside of the seat blank. It's held at the front edge and centered from side to side.

Place the bridge on the support blocks with the indexing pins in the No. 1 bridge holes.

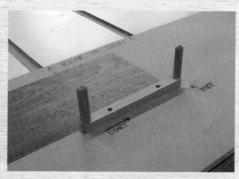

With the guide block placed against the left-hand stop of the travel groove, everything is ready to begin the first pass of the scoop.

After the first pass is made, the saw blade is raised to $1/4$" and the process is repeated. The result is a clean scoop.

Once the guide block reaches the right stop, it is pivoted in the V-notch in a counterclockwise rotation. After the pivot, the guide block is pushed to the right travel stop to complete the first pass.

After the series of passes are made, the seat is fully scooped. The blank is then sanded or scraped to remove any milling marks.

reaches the right stop of the travel groove. This places the opposite end of the guide block at the centered V-notch.

6. Slowly and carefully engage the end of the guide block in the V-notch by turning the guide block in a counterclockwise direction. Rotate the block and seat blank 180°, making a complete U-turn.

7. With the front edge of the seat now facing left, continue moving the guide block along the travel groove back to the right stop. The first pass is complete.

8. Raise the blade to establish the full depth of cut ($1/4$") and repeat the process. For a seat such as mine, the $1/4$" blade height will be all the depth needed. You can leave the blade set here for the rest of the scooping process because each successive pass now makes a slight cut, expanding the width of the previous pass.

9. With the left side of the bridge still engaged in hole 1 L, move the right side of the bridge to hole 2 R and repeat the cutting operation.

10. Now move the bridge to holes 2 L and 2 R and repeat the operation again. Then move the bridge to holes 3 L and 2 R. By advancing the bridge in this staggered progression to higher-numbered holes (up to 10), the width of the saddling is increased.

During the scooping process, interrupt the operation periodically to clear accumulating dust from the jig base as needed.

The saddled seat will be mildly scarred by saw blade marks. These are easily and quickly removed with sandpaper or a card scraper once the blank has been completely scooped.

First Make the Jig

There are seven relatively simple pieces that make up the jig needed for this technique. All of them can be built in the shop using common materials you probably already have on hand.

Let's start with the jig's base that clamps to the table saw and is 36" wide × 32" deep (you may need to alter the size to fit your saw).

With the blade all the way down, secure the MDF to the saw. Start the saw and slowly raise the blade through the base about $3/8$" above the MDF. Remove the base and drill a series of $1/2$"-diameter holes around the saw cut to facilitate sawdust collection. Based on the location of the saw cut, draw a line perpendicular to the apex of the saw blade's height.

Next, make and install the two bridge support blocks. (These blocks should hold the bridge high enough to clear the thickness of the seat blank as it travels between the bridge and the base.) In the center of the top edge of the blocks, drill

Support blocks elevate the bridge and provide space for the seat blank. The indexing pins are used with the holes at each end of the bridge.

The bridge is central to the scooping operation. Its travel groove controls the path of the seat blank and the V-notch (inset) is the pivot point for making the U-turn.

a $\frac{1}{4}$"-diameter hole and tap a $\frac{1}{4}$" steel pin into each block. (Leave about $\frac{3}{4}$" of the pin above the block.) Carefully install the blocks on the jig base so the center of the pin aligns with your apex line (see the drawing on page 123).

Build a Bridge

The bridge is a critical part of the jig. It controls the width and length of the scoop (the depth is controlled by the height of the saw blade). The bridge extends across the table saw and is approximately $6\frac{1}{2}$" wide and as long as the width of your jig's base. Centered

along its length is a $\frac{1}{2}$"- deep × 16"-long cutout that I call the "travel groove." Centered on the travel groove is a $\frac{3}{8}$"-wide V-notch. At each end of the bridge is a series of 10 $\frac{1}{4}$"-diameter holes, spaced $\frac{1}{2}$" from center to center. These holes must be spaced side to side so that the bridge will drop onto the $\frac{1}{4}$" pins in the bridge support blocks.

Make the Guide Block

The guide block is screwed to the underside of your seat blank and slides along the travel groove in the bridge. It also provides handles for pushing the seat blank along, and is used to make the pivot motion in the V-notch of the travel groove. It is this pivot that swings the blank 180° to finish its trip along the

travel groove. Make the guide block taller than the top edge of the travel groove when the guide is mounted to the bottom of seat blank (2" in this example).

At each end of the block are dowels used for handles. These handles need to extend at least $1\frac{1}{2}$" above the block – long enough to provide a secure grip for the operator while guiding the seat blank along the bridge's travel groove. The guide block is mounted perpendicular to and flush with the front edge of the seat blank, and it's centered side to side.

That's all there is to the jig, and it's one you can use over and over as long as your seat blank thickness fits between the jig base and bridge. Step up to your saw. You're ready to start scooping seats the quick and easy way.

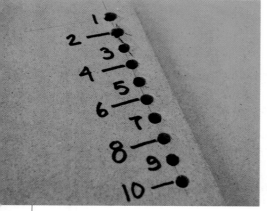

Both ends of the bridge have $\frac{1}{4}$" holes set on $\frac{1}{2}$" centers that are used to position the bridge on the support pins.

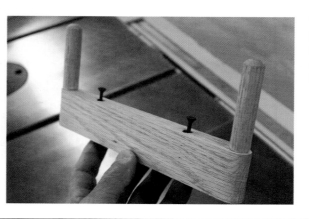

The guide block attaches to the bottom of the seat and controls the blank's travel along the bridge. Dowels serve as handles.

Furniture Fundamentals: Chairs & Benches. Copyright © 2014 by Popular Woodworking. Printed and bound in the USA. All rights reserved. No part of this book may be reproduced in any form or by any electronic or mechanical means including information storage and retrieval systems without permission in writing from the publisher, except by a reviewer, who may quote brief passages in a review. Published by Popular Woodworking Books, an imprint of F+W, A Content + eCommerce Company, 10151 Carver Rd. Blue Ash, Ohio, 45236. (800) 289-0963. First edition.

Distributed in Canada by Fraser Direct
100 Armstrong Avenue
Georgetown, Ontario L7G 5S4
Canada

Distributed in the U.K. and Europe by
F+W Media International, LTD
Brunel House, Ford Close
Newton Abbot
TQ12 4PU, UK
Tel: (+44) 1626 323200
Fax: (+44) 1626 323319

Distributed in Australia by Capricorn Link
P.O. Box 704
Windsor, NSW 2756
Australia

Visit our website at popularwoodworking.com or our consumer website at shopwoodworking.com for more woodworking information projects.

Other fine Popular Woodworking Books are available from your local bookstore or direct from the publisher.

ISBN-13: 978-1-4403-4051-2

18   17   16   15   14   5   4   3   2   1

Editor: Robert W. Lang
Designer: Daniel T. Pessell
Production coordinator: Debbie Thomas

About the Authors

CHUCK BENDER
Chuck is a former senior editor with *Popular Woodworking Magazine*; he has been a professional woodworker for several decades.

ADAM CHERUBINI
Adam is a former contributing editor with *Popular Woodworking Magazine* and was the founding author of the magazine's Arts & Mysteries column.

BERT JOHANSEN
Bert is an amateur woodworker and former NASA engineer.

ROBERT W. LANG
Bob is a former executive editor with *Popular Woodworking Magazine* and has been a professional woodworker since the early 1970s.

OWEN REIN
Owen lives in Stone County, Ark., where he continues to make rocking chairs as well as split baskets.

MARIO RODRIGUEZ
Mario has more than 30 years' experience as woodworker, teacher and writer. He now is co-owner of the Philadelphia Furniture Workshop.

GARY ROGOWSKI
Gary is the director of the Northwest Woodworking School in Portland, Ore. He's been building furniture since 1974.

CHRISTOPHER SCHWARZ
Chris is a former editor of *Popular Woodworking Magazine* (now contributing editor) and is the editor at Lost Art Press.

JIM STACK
Jim is a former senior editor of *Popular Woodworking Books* and is the author of eight woodworking books.

JIM STUARD
Jim was associate editor of *Popular Woodworking Magazine* for a number of years and has now gone over to the genteel world of fly fishing.

MICHELLE TAUTE
Michelle is a former associate editor with *Popular Woodworking Magazine* and is now a freelance writer and editor.

DAVID THIEL
David is a former senior editor of *Popular Woodworking Magazine* and now works with books and videos under the *Popular Woodworking* brand.

KARA GEBHART UHL
Kara was managing editor of *Popular Woodworking Magazine* for four years, learning woodworking skills along the way. She is currently a freelance writer and editor.

Metric Conversion Chart

TO CONVERT	TO	MULTIPLY BY
Inches	Centimeters	2.54
Centimeters	Inches	0.4
Feet	Centimeters	30.5
Centimeters	Feet	0.03
Yards	Meters	0.9
Meters	Yards	1.1

Read This Important Safety Notice

To prevent accidents, keep safety in mind while you work. Use the safety guards installed on power equipment; they are for your protection.

When working on power equipment, keep fingers away from saw blades, wear safety goggles to prevent injuries from flying wood chips and sawdust, wear hearing protection and consider installing a dust vacuum to reduce the amount of airborne sawdust in your woodshop.

Don't wear loose clothing, such as neckties or shirts with loose sleeves, or jewelry, such as rings, necklaces or bracelets, when working on power equipment. Tie back long hair to prevent it from getting caught in your equipment.

People who are sensitive to certain chemicals should check the chemical content of any product before using it.

Due to the variability of local conditions, construction materials, skill levels, etc., neither the author nor Popular Woodworking Books assumes any responsibility for any accidents, injuries, damages or other losses incurred resulting from the material presented in this book.

The authors and editors who compiled this book have tried to make the contents as accurate and correct as possible. Plans, illustrations, photographs and text have been carefully checked. All instructions, plans and projects should be carefully read, studied and understood before beginning construction.

Prices listed for supplies and equipment were current at the time of publication and are subject to change.

IDEAS • INSTRUCTION • INSPIRATION

These are other great Popular Woodworking products are available at your local bookstore, woodworking store or online supplier.

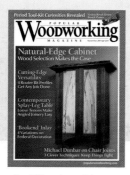

Popular Woodworking Magazine

Get must-build projects, information on tools (both hand and power) and their use and technique instruction in every issue of *Popular Woodworking Magazine.* Each issue (7 per year) includes articles and expert information from some of the best-known names in woodworking. Subscribe today at popularwoodworking.com.

Subscription • 7 issues/year

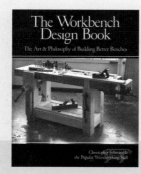

The Workbench Design Book
By Christopher Schwarz

How many times have you heard this: "The workbench is the most important tool in your shop." While the statement is absolutely true, it doesn't help you answer the more important question: Which workbench should you build? This book explores that problem and detail you won't find in any other source in print or online.

Hardcover • 256 pages

Hybrid Woodworking
By Marc Spagnuolo

Known online as The Wood Whisperer, Marc Spaguolo presents a fresh approach to woodworking and furniture making by showing the most efficient ways to utilize both power tools and hand tools in the furniture building process. Not only will you learn which tools are best for which tasks, but you will also find tips for how to use, maintain, and fine tune them.

Paperback • 192 pages

Ultimate Workshop Solutions
By Popular Woodworking Editors

From better clamp storage, to the perfect miter saw stand to benches and beyond, you'll find 35 projects specifically designed to improve and organize your favorite space. These projects have been created by the editors of *Popular Woodworking Magazine* for your shop, and now we're pleased to share them with you.

Paperback • 192 pages

Basic Sketch-Up For Woodworkers
By Joe Zeh

SketchUp has helped thousands of woodworkers create, correct and perfect their furniture designs before the first piece of expensive wood is cut. Now Joe Zeh, an expert in Sketchup and Computer-Aided Design (CAD) will show you the brand-new 2014 edition and how much easier and more versatile it is to use.

**Available at Shopwoodworking.com
DVD**

Joinery Master Class With Frank Klausz
By Frank Klausz

Frank Klausz, expert craftsmen and experienced woodworking teacher, shares with you on this 2-DVD set the joinery skills he's learned in a lifetime (edge-joint options, bridle joints, dovetails, mortise-and-tenon variations and more!). Plus five projects to help you put your joinery knowledge into practice.

**Available at Shopwoodworking.com
DVD & download**

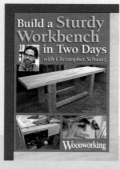

Build A Sturdy Workbench In Two Days
By Christopher Schwarz

With a base built from standard 4x4 lumber, a base with half-lap construction, and a top made from two IKEA countertops, this two-day workbench is a seriously sturdy shop workhorse that no one will question for quality. With this solid workbench, you'll have no shortage of working surface or dog holes.

**Available at Shopwoodworking.com
DVD & download**

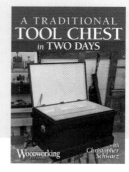

A Traditional Tool Chest In Two Days
By Christopher Schwarz

Woodworkers who use traditional tool chests swear they're the most convenient way to organize tools. Now, you can make one in just two days using modern materials and contemporary joinery techniques. Whether your focus is hand tool or power tool woodworking, you'll find this tool chest indispensable (a quick to build!).

**Available at Shopwoodworking.com
DVD & download**

Visit **popularwoodworking.com** to see more woodworking information by the experts, learn about our digital subscription and sign up to receive our free newsletter or blog posts.